# Multinational Corporation Subsidiaries in China

# CHANDOS
## ASIAN STUDIES SERIES:
### CONTEMPORARY ISSUES AND TRENDS

Series Editor: Professor Chris Rowley,
Centre for Research on Asian Management, Cass Business School,
City University, UK; HEAD Foundation, Singapore
(email: c.rowley@city.ac.uk)

Chandos Publishing is pleased to publish this major Series of books entitled *Asian Studies: Contemporary Issues and Trends*. The Series Editor is Professor Chris Rowley, Director, Centre for Research on Asian Management, City University, UK and Director, Research and Publications, HEAD Foundation, Singapore.

Asia has clearly undergone some major transformations in recent years and books in the Series examine this transformation from a number of perspectives: economic, management, social, political and cultural. We seek authors from a broad range of areas and disciplinary interests: covering, for example, business/management, political science, social science, history, sociology, gender studies, ethnography, economics and international relations, etc.

Importantly, the Series examines both current developments and possible future trends. The Series is aimed at an international market of academics and professionals working in the area. The books have been specially commissioned from leading authors. The objective is to provide the reader with an authoritative view of current thinking.

**New authors**: we would be delighted to hear from you if you have an idea for a book. We are interested in both shorter, practically orientated publications (45,000+ words) and longer, theoretical monographs (75,000–100,000 words). Our books can be single, joint or multi-author volumes. If you have an idea for a book, please contact the publishers or Professor Chris Rowley, the Series Editor.

Dr Glyn Jones
Chandos Publishing
Email: gjones@chandospublishing.com
www.chandospublishing.com

Professor Chris Rowley
Cass Business School, City University
Email: c.rowley@city.ac.uk
www.cass.city.ac.uk/faculty/c.rowley

**Chandos Publishing**: Chandos Publishing is an imprint of Woodhead Publishing Limited. The aim of Chandos Publishing is to publish books of the highest possible standard: books that are both intellectually stimulating and innovative.

We are delighted and proud to count our authors from such well known international organisations as the Asian Institute of Technology, Tsinghua University, Kookmin University, Kobe University, Kyoto Sangyo University, London School of Economics, University of Oxford, Michigan State University, Getty Research Library, University of Texas at Austin, University of South Australia, University of Newcastle, Australia, University of Melbourne, ILO, Max-Planck Institute, Duke University and the leading law firm Clifford Chance.

A key feature of Chandos Publishing's activities is the service it offers its authors and customers. Chandos Publishing recognises that its authors are at the core of its publishing ethos, and authors are treated in a friendly, efficient and timely manner. Chandos Publishing's books are marketed on an international basis, via its range of overseas agents and representatives.

**Professor Chris Rowley**: Dr Rowley, BA, MA (Warwick), DPhil (Nuffield College, Oxford) is Subject Group leader and the inaugural Professor of Human Resource Management at Cass Business School, City University, London, UK, and Director of Research and Publications for the HEAD Foundation, Singapore. He is the founding Director of the multi-disciplinary and internationally networked Centre for Research on Asian Management (http://www.cass.city.ac.uk/cram/index.html) and Editor of the leading journal *Asia Pacific Business Review* (www.tandf.co.uk/journals/titles/13602381.asp). He is well known and highly regarded in the area, with visiting appointments at leading Asian universities and top journal Editorial Boards in the UK, Asia and the US. He has given a range of talks and lectures to universities, companies and organisations internationally with research and consultancy experience with unions, business and government, and his previous employment includes varied work in both the public and private sectors. Professor Rowley researches in a range of areas, including international and comparative human resource management and Asia Pacific management and business. He has been awarded grants from the British Academy, an ESRC AIM International Study Fellowship and gained a 5-year RCUK Fellowship in Asian Business and Management. He acts as a reviewer for many funding bodies, as well as for numerous journals and publishers. Professor Rowley publishes extensively, including in leading US and UK journals, with over 370 articles, books, chapters and other contributions.

**Bulk orders**: some organisations buy a number of copies of our books. If you are interested in doing this, we would be pleased to discuss a discount. Please email wp@ woodheadpublishing.com or telephone +44 (0) 1223 499140.

# Multinational Corporation Subsidiaries in China

*An empirical study of growth and development strategy*

JINGHUA ZHAO, JIFU WANG,
VIPIN GUPTA AND TIM HUDSON

**CP**

CHANDOS
PUBLISHING

Oxford Cambridge Philadelphia New Delhi

Chandos Publishing
Hexagon House
Avenue 4
Station Lane
Witney
Oxford OX28 4BN
UK
Tel: +44 (0) 1993 848726
Email: info@chandospublishing.com
www.chandospublishing.com

Chandos Publishing is an imprint of Woodhead Publishing Limited

Woodhead Publishing Limited
80 High Street
Sawston
Cambridge CB22 3HJ
UK
Tel: +44 (0) 1223 499140
Fax: + 44 (0) 1223 832819
www.woodheadpublishing.com

---

First published in 2012

ISBN: 978-0-08-101684-8 (print) (Chandos Publishing)

ISBN: 978-0-85709-163-5 (print) (Woodhead Publishing)

ISBN: 978-1-78063-333-6 (online)

British Library Cataloguing-in-Publication Data.
A catalogue record for this book is available from the British Library.

Printed in the UK and USA.

# Contents

# List of figures and tables

## Figures

# Tables

# About the authors

**Jinghua Zhao** (PhD from Nanjing University) is a professor in strategy and the dean of the School of Government at China Central University of Finance and Economics. His research focus is on strategy in multinational companies (MNCs) and government. He has published more than 50 journal articles and 7 books.

**Jifu Wang** (PhD from Auburn University) is an associate professor at the School of Business Administration of the University of Houston. He was the president of US Geneses Global Capital and the chairman of Lanfu Global LLC before he came back to the academic world in spring 2012. He functioned as acting dean, management department chair and an associate professor at the School of Business Administration of the University of Houston, Victoria, for more than 10 years. He also served as an executive in top management teams for several group companies in China's Shenzhen Special Economic Zone and has rich management experience and skills in international business. His research interest includes global strategy and organisational change, and he has published 36 refereed journal articles and several books and book chapters in global strategy with focus on core competence and capable organisations.

**Vipin Gupta** (PhD from Wharton School) is a professor and co-director, Global Management Center at the College of Business and Public Administration, California State University, San Bernardino. He has published more than 125 refereed journal articles and book chapters, and several books, focused on three research streams. First, the dynamic modelling of technological growth and organisational performance, transformation and sustainability, incorporating global and local factors, and trading and human factors – the subject of his PhD dissertation, as well as his two books and a strategy textbook. Second, analysis of societal and organisational cultures, the ontology and epistemology of cultural influences on individual, corporate, national and regional level behaviours and development, and the role of institutions, strategy and policy in cultural and gender inclusion – he is the principal co-investigator and co-author of the award-winning GLOBE project on culture and leadership in 62 societies. Third, analysis of how culture influences family business models in different regions of the world – he has lead-edited 11 books on this theme.

**Tim Hudson** (PhD from Clark University) is the vice chancellor of the Texas Tech University system. He was the president of the University of Houston, Victoria, for six years. His research interests include international development, globalisation and cultural aspects of markets, international education and leadership. He is a member of the International Association of University Presidents. He has conducted research, worked and led student groups in more than 40 countries around the world. He received an honorary doctorate from London Guildhall University for his lifetime commitment to fostering international understanding.

# Part 1
# Overview and conceptual
# building blocks

# Introduction

**Abstract:** In this chapter, we discuss the need for new empirical research on the growth and development strategy of multinational corporation (MNC) subsidiaries in China. We explain the purpose of the new research reported in this book.

**Key words:** MNC subsidiaries, growth and development strategy, empirical research, MNCs in China.

## Need for this study

Multinational corporations heavily influence the strategy of their overseas subsidiaries. Several studies have investigated the relationship between MNC overseas subsidiaries and their parent companies (Bartlett and Ghosha, 1986; Jarillo and Martinez, 1990; Prahalad and Doz, 1987; Taggart, 1996; Gupta and Govindarajan, 1991; Birkinshaw and Morrison, 1995). A common element of these studies is a focus on how overseas subsidiaries handle the pressures and the balance between globalisation needs and local demand while formulating their strategy.

With the increasing importance of subsidiaries' function and contribution in the overall development of MNCs, the study of subsidiaries' enterprise development has been of great recent interest (Pan and Lu, 2003). Perspectives such as enterprise network theory, resource-based theory and enterprise development theory have been applied to study interactive relationships between subsidiaries and their external and internal environments (Birkinshaw and Hood, 1997, 1998).

In the late twentieth century, many MNCs began to establish subsidiaries in China. In the Chinese context, the emphasis of the studies on enterprise development has been on: 1) small and medium-sized enterprise growth (Gu, 2000); 2) family enterprise development, particularly entrepreneurial capability change in the process of organisation growth and succession (Wu, Jia and Chen, 2003); 3) product life cycle management (Zhang, 2003); 4) new century modes for enterprise development (Li, 2002); 5) digital modes for enterprise development (Du and Tang, 2002); and 6) entrepreneurial spirit and capability (Li, 2002; Liu and Chen, 2001). Most of these research studies have a macro focus, such as MNC investment in China, enterprise structure and the impact on the national economy. A few studies have a micro focus, such as subsidiary strategies, subsidiary operations and subsidiary management; yet these studies are mostly descriptive. There is a scarcity of empirical analyses at the micro level for MNC subsidiaries' growth and development strategy in China. The present study fills this gap.

The study of MNCs' overseas subsidiaries began more than 20 years ago in the 1970s, with studies such as those conducted by Youssef and Hulbert (1975). The subsequent literature on MNCs overseas subsidiaries' growth and developmental strategy can be organised into four genres of studies: strategy-structure, headquarter-subsidiary relationship, subsidiary role and subsidiary development. After reviewing this literature, we propose that the growth and development strategy system for multinational overseas subsidiaries is formed by three layers: corporate strategy, system strategy and functional strategy. We empirically analyse the tactics for growth and development in each layer.

We investigate MNC subsidiaries' horizontal and vertical behavioural trends. Horizontal trends involve various countries, industries and roles, while vertical trends suggest time sequences of growth and development strategies. From the horizontal angle, the model compares common and specific features of MNC subsidiaries in China based on country of origin and industry of operation. From the vertical point of view, the model analyses the evolutionary process in which MNC subsidiaries in China have changed their strategic system, strategic tendency and strategic intent and describes the stages for their evolution. The strategic evolution model provides a rational framework for comprehensive theoretical analysis of MNC subsidiaries in China.

At present, most MNC studies in China use second-hand materials, data and other sources with very low empirical validity. In order to obtain a more objective understanding, we use a questionnaire survey to obtain first-hand information. We summarise new features of these subsidiaries that have emerged in recent years.

## Practical significance of this study

Like other Chinese firms, the multinational subsidiaries in China are facing a tough issue: how to achieve continual growth and development. The ancient Chinese wisdom teaches that only when we know ourselves and our rivals very well can we eventually win the war.

With expansion of MNC investment in China, global competition in the Chinese market is increasing and becoming fierce. Multinational subsidiaries in China are from different countries and are competing in different industries. They face different challenges in the global marketplace, in host-country policies and in the level of competition in the local market. They exhibit distinct personality characteristics, generating diverse strategies for growth and development. These diverse growth and development strategies manifest themselves in variations in such significant factors as strategic motives, roles and behaviours of MNC subsidiaries.

The growth and development strategies for MNC subsidiaries in China are a function of two major factors: first, the implementation of the global strategic mission of the parent firm; second, their own need for growth and development in China. With the persistently high growth of the Chinese economy and improved global positioning of China, many multinational corporations have defined China as a strategic platform for their global operations.

In the early years, MNCs' subsidiaries in China behaved more like a foreign-owned entity. Increasingly, however, these subsidiaries have evolved to give more attention to corporate social responsibility. Simultaneously, the so-called gregarious growth models have gradually emerged. These evolutions engender several questions on the strategies adopted by MNC subsidiaries in China:

- What is the position of China in the global strategy system of MNCs?

- How have MNCs repositioned in the Chinese market, and what is the strategy of their Chinese subsidiaries?

- What influence do the subsidiaries have on the evolution of strategic positioning, strategic intent and strategic direction for MNCs?

- What are the new features of the functional strategies of these subsidiaries?

Chinese enterprises are still not in a position to start an all-round competition with MNCs. In 2003, only seven Chinese firms were ranked among the world's most competitive enterprises in Fortune 500. They were largely focused on monopolistic industries, including edible oil, petrochemicals and telecommunications. Comparative studies can help local Chinese firms better understand strategic content and operational orientations of MNC subsidiaries in their industry and take corresponding countermeasures.

MNCs have exerted tremendous impact on the growth and development of Chinese enterprises. Their subsidiaries offer two significant practical values to these Chinese firms: benchmarks for local operations and best practice for international expansion. Chinese enterprises can also understand the effects of various strategic choices of operations at different time periods with different industries. They can identify the strategic evolutionary process of transnational operations in different stages, so that they may also effectively manage their subsidiaries in other countries for global competition.

As China has opened up, the number of foreign subsidiaries has rapidly increased and created continuous expansion in the region. All adjustments to the investment strategy of MNC subsidiaries impacts China's economic growth and industrial development, both domestically and globally. Comparative studies can assist the Chinese government in formulating appropriate laws and regulations, guiding leading MNC subsidiaries in China and assuring that the latter conform to China's laws and customs. The Chinese government can also gain insights to formulate reasonable regulations and policies to guide Chinese subsidiaries in different industries. The methodologies applied to govern multinational subsidiaries are a significant benchmark for the Chinese government in making policy for regulating and guiding MNC subsidiaries operating in China. Therefore, the findings of this study have great practical value when used to identify or construct fundamental economic policies.

## Purpose and methods

The purposes of this book are:

- to review and compare theories on the growth and development strategy of MNC overseas subsidiaries, in the context of MNC subsidiaries in China, through empirical research;

- to compare and analyse the evolution, life cycle, growth path and growth strategy of MNC subsidiaries in China;

- to compare and analyse the development strategy system of MNC subsidiaries in China on marketing, research and development (R&D) and human resource functions;

- to compare and analyse the motives and characteristics of strategic change and adjustment in multinational subsidiaries in China.

The ultimate objective of this study is to investigate the competitive advantages of Chinese multinational subsidiaries and analyse how they have cultivated their own core competencies to achieve self-sustained growth as domestic enterprises. Such an investigation will offer strategic recommendations and the theory and reference guide for China's macro and micro decision-making policies (enterprise level, industrial level and government level).

These objectives are met through two types of study: literature review and empirical analysis.

The literature review encompasses studies of strategic management theory, international growth strategy, production integration and globalisation processes, and comparisons across different countries or regions. It includes a review of both Chinese as well as international literature.

A survey of a representative sample of MNC subsidiaries in China is used to conduct statistical analyses. Vertical comparisons across time periods, and horizontal comparisons across different industrial sectors and national origins, along with functional analysis, add to the analytical depth and uniqueness. The focus of this study is on both horizontal and vertical comparisons in different countries, different industries and inside the global area with the growth and development strategies of multinational Chinese subsidiaries.

# 2

# Conceptual building blocks

**Abstract:** In this chapter, we review the core conceptual building blocks for the research conducted in this book. The building blocks focus on the growth and development strategy of MNC overseas subsidiaries and the role and functional strategies of MNC overseas subsidiaries. They also include strategy, based on the SWOT model, and strategic evolution of MNC overseas subsidiaries.

**Key words:** MNC overseas subsidiaries, growth and development strategy, strategic choice, strategy evolution.

## Multinational corporations (MNCs)

The concept of the MNC has a very broad meaning. Traditionally, the definition of MNCs tends to be concentrated mainly in structural standards, such as those adopted in the form of the trans-border distribution, production or service facilities, and as an extension of the parent corporation's domestic operations. With globalisation, distinctions among businesses, countries and marketing are becoming increasingly blurred, thereby generating an evolution in the concept of the MNC. Contractor and Lorange (1988) note, 'traditionally, multinational corporations can be viewed as a transnational force of nature, the enterprises' own internal control chain, but in today's complicated, competitive world, it should be seen as quasi-market transactions inter-dependent on each

11

other.' Both organisational theory and organisational behaviour factors are becoming important in conceptualising MNCs. Perlmutter (1969), for instance, notes how the values and modes of behaviour of the MNCs usually evolve in three stages: orientation of home country, orientation of host country and orientation of the world. Perlmutter believes that an enterprise can be considered truly a multinational corporation only when it enters the 'orientation of the world'.

According to the United Nations Commission on Multinational Corporations, MNCs are 'companies that set up headquarters in another country or region, by two or more countries in the form of public entities, or through private or mixed-ownership enterprises. They have the following common characteristics: (1) they share the title as a link to connect to each other; (2) they rely on the resources in common, such as currency and credit, information systems, trademarks, patents, and technology, etc; (3) they are controlled by a common strategy' (Zhao, 1996).

For the purposes of this study, the definition of MNCs includes two major aspects: (1) MNCs set up their headquarters in one country and, through direct investments in two or more countries, they set up branches or subsidiaries in the enterprise system; (2) MNCs have a global operational strategy – they endeavour to maximise the overall benefit of synergetic efforts while maintaining a global strategic system as their target, instead of a one-sided pursuit of the best interests of a particular nation.

## MNC subsidiaries

When a parent MNC invests directly in a host country, it creates a local subsidiary that has a filial relationship to the parent company (Teng, Huang and Zhang, 1992). Foreign subsidiaries are an extension of the parent MNC, entrusted to achieve specific goals. The concept of MNC subsidiaries has a legal dimension beyond the filial concept in that they are also an individual entity that must operate under the laws of the host country. The subsidiaries have certain autonomy in management and have independent legal status.

A parent MNC maintains strategic control over the subsidiaries in three major ways: equity, organisation and knowledge (Yang, 2000). Organisational control and knowledge control are usually predicated on leveraging securities and shares. The manner in which the parent company exercises equity control over the subsidiary – such as wholly or partially owned structure or joint venture – determines the amount of influence the parent company can exert. Theoretically speaking, an MNC that owns a majority 51 per cent or more of the equity of a subsidiary is able to acquire absolute control. In practice, dispersion of ownership and the diversification of investors allow control with much less than a majority interest of the shares. In all cases, the MNC can also control and coordinate the production and business activities of subsidiaries through many additional means, including strategy, culture, human resources, marketing and financial systems. The parent MNCs also frame and enact strategic direction of their subsidiaries through perpetual executive intervention.

## Growth and development strategy system

In this book, the focus is on the strategy of growth and development of multinational subsidiaries. The focus is on the ability of these overseas subsidiaries to invest in the sustainable development of the host country, through strategic choices that consider external and internal environmental factors and resource availability. These choices are both gradually coordinated from the higher levels of business's hierarchy as well as integrated into the lower levels of the strategic system. The subsidiary growth and development strategic system comprises three synergic levels: corporate, operational and functional.

## Corporate-level role of MNC subsidiaries

The overseas subsidiaries of MNCs are controlled by the parent company, while simultaneously engaging in a complex relationship with other subsidiaries and affiliate subsidiaries. Their role is a function of the MNCs' global network system and is responsible for matching the internal and external resources within this system and exercising specific functions aligned with these resources. The strategic motive of the parent MNC prescribes the strategic mission for the subsidiary and defines certain roles for them, right from the initial and early set-up stage. From the internal analysis of network systems, the subsidiaries have different strategic positions and roles in an MNC network system. The strategic positions are defined by competitive ability and other variances among subsidiary resources. These varying positions are associated with the differences in their global strategy, showing different strategic autonomy, priorities in resource allocation and varying degrees of dependence on the parent company.

## Operational strategies of MNC subsidiaries

The complex corporate-level role of the subsidiaries makes their strategic choice of organisations–environment analysis different from the usual analysis. Therefore, to identify operational strategies or strategic posture of MNC subsidiaries,

**Figure 2.1**   SWOT analyses for general business

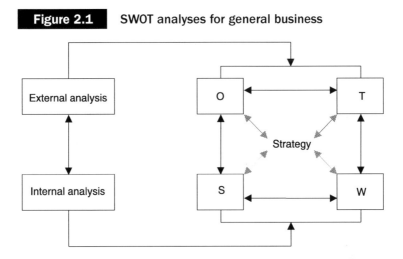

it is useful to conduct subsidiary SWOT – identifying the strengths, weaknesses, opportunities and threats of the subsidiary (S-SWOT). Figure 2.1 shows the relationship between S-SWOT analysis and strategy, highlighting four operational choices for growth and development strategy.

## 1 Strength–opportunity (SO) strategy

The SO strategy works if the enterprise has many external opportunities and a powerful internal advantage. It depends on the internal advantage of a company and its utilisation of external opportunities. If an enterprise has abundant capital, advanced technology and a highly skilled workforce, it should find a market in a country with great development potential and adopt the SO strategy to carve out this new foreign market.

## 2 Weakness–opportunity (WO) strategy

The WO strategy works if an enterprise has external opportunity but a weak internal system. It stabilises development using the external opportunity to ameliorate the internal disadvantage. An enterprise that is faced with growth in market demand but that lacks technical resources should adopt this strategy.

## 3 Weakness–threat (WT) strategy

The WT strategy works to improve a poor internal situation, avoid threat and eliminate disadvantages of the external environment. It directly overcomes internal disadvantages and avoids external threat. It helps an enterprise to strengthen internal management and improve product quality.

## 4 Strength–threat (ST) strategy

The ST strategy works if an enterprise has internal advantage, but faces external threat. It is a strategy of diversification into new markets, to leverage internal advantage and avoid external threats. For example, a pharmaceutical company has strong capital and many marketing channels; however, when domestic demand has gradually shrunk, it should adopt the ST strategy to drive operational growth through the diversification process to decentralised operational risks.

## *Functional strategies of MNC subsidiaries*

This study focuses on three strategic functions: marketing, human resource, and research and development (R&D).

Marketing strategy function includes the marketing strategy's posture and tropism, competitive marketing strategy, blueprint and marketing combination, blueprint of the subsidiaries, and marketing strategy as a guide to marketing tactics and strategies to implement.

Human resources strategy function is a game plan to develop plans and methods for human talents, to implement such measures and to achieve the strategic goals of the enterprise through human resource management activities. As Wiseman and Gomez-Mejia (1998) noted: 'enterprises' careful use of human resources is to help enterprises to obtain and maintain their competitive advantage; it is a plan or method to organise the effective activities of the staff to achievement of the organisational goals.' Human resource strategy functions include recruitment, selection, pay, training and development, and performance evaluation. The human resource strategy of MNC subsidiaries works at two levels: the vertical interactions between the parent or holding company and its subsidiaries; and the horizontal interactions among subsidiaries within the enterprise group. The vertical interactions between the parent and its subsidiary companies are guided by the human resource policies of the parent corporation, along with investment motivation factors, and by the strategy tropism, role and resource allocation of the overseas subsidiaries. The horizontal interactions among the subsidiaries are usually associated with the MNC competitive strategy and its relation with the MNC human resource management strategy.

The R&D strategy of overseas subsidiaries refers to subsidiaries' initiatives for their own development, or actions for following the strategic requirements of the global R&D network system of the parent company through the establishment of R&D institutions. It includes allocation of R&D resources including investment in R&D funding, recruitment and training. Multinational subsidiaries are involved in R&D to win sustainable competitive advantage via mapping of future strategic moves.

## Strategy evolution of MNC subsidiaries

Changes in global industry and national macroeconomic environment impact the demand for organisational resources, internal networks and accepted roles within an MNC network system and generate strategy evolution of MNC subsidiaries in terms of strategic characteristics, abilities and positions.

Figure 2.2 summarises the analytical model based on the conceptual building blocks.

**Figure 2.2** Analytical model of MNC subsidiary strategy system

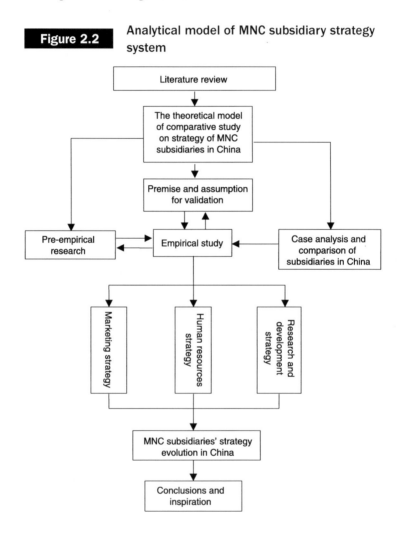

# Part 2
# Theoretical background and methodology

# 3

# Theoretical background

**Abstract:** In this chapter, we review literature on MNC development strategies, including the study of MNC strategic management theory, MNC growth and development strategy, and cross-country perspectives. We also review works on the strategy of MNC overseas subsidiaries, including strategy–structure theory, the studies on the relationship between the parent and subsidiary companies, and the studies on subsidiaries' development.

**Key words:** MNC development strategies, MNC strategic management, strategy–structure theory, parent company, subsidiaries.

The theory of MNCs originated in response to the rapid development of Western multinational corporations after the Second World War (Hymer, 1996; Dunning, 1977; Lin, 1984). The study of MNC subsidiaries has become an important field of study since the 1980s. The focus has been on MNC strategies and structure (Stopford and Wells, 1972), the relationship between the parent and subsidiary companies (Prahalad and Doz, 1987), the roles of the subsidiaries (Bartlett and Ghoshal, 1986), and the development of subsidiaries (Birkinshaw and Hood, 1998a, 1998b). Given the rapid growth of MNCs in China, there is a need to re-examine these theories and analyses in light of the experiences of the MNC subsidiaries in China.

# Evolution of MNC theory

After the Second World War, Western MNCs developed rapidly. The classical international trade theory failed to explain these developments. Western scholars studying MNCs gradually developed different schools of explanations, starting with the monopoly theory of Stephen H. Hymer in the early 1960s. Three phases of development in theoretical schools are identifiable.

The first phase, from the early 1960s to the mid-1970s, offered explanations of the characteristics and the influencing factors of foreign direct investment of MNCs from different countries. Based on the analysis of US firms' overseas expansion, the explanations focused on monopoly competitive advantages and product life cycle. Beginning at the end of the 1960s with the expansion of foreign direct investment development in Western Europe and Japan, scholars of those countries, such as Kojima in Japan, began making important theoretical contributions.

The second phase, from the mid-1970s through the early 1980s, produced a shift towards a general theory of MNCs, such as internalisation theory and eclectic theory. The research purpose was to show that different countries have different sectors of foreign direct investment activities.

The third phase, starting from the mid-1980s, was inspired by the rapid challenges of technological revolution. MNCs implemented new global business strategies and formed strategic alliances to adapt to the global competitive environment. The focus of the research shifted to the management of strategic alliances.

In general, MNC theories seek to explain three factors: first, MNC strategic management; second, MNC integrated growth and development strategy; and third, distinctive features of the Japanese MNC strategy.

## *MNC strategic management theory*

### Focus on MNC development strategy

MNC strategic management theory has its roots in the early 1970s. In the book entitled *Managing Multinational Enterprises*, American scholars Stopford and Wells (1972) explored the link between two strategic variables – export ratios and the diversification of export – and organisational structures, and thus expanded Chandler's research on strategic organisation and organisational structure (Chandler, 1962) to the international arena. In the 1980s, Ghoshal and other scholars[1] investigated dynamic adjustment and mutual accommodation among the three factors: environment, strategy and organisational structure. The MNC strategy was identified as choosing or creating an environment where MNCs can use their unique competitive advantages. The accomplishment of such a strategy was seen as a function of highly appropriate coordination among firm objectives, policies and various functional departments.

Michael Porter (1986, 1990)[2] used the concept of value chain to describe the MNC's strategic structure and source of competitive advantage. He identified MNC strategy in terms of two strategic variables: first, the integration of business activities and strategic positioning worldwide; and second, the coordination of activities in different countries along the MNC value chain. The scope of integration shows changes between centralisation and decentralisation. Coordination is a matter of aligning operations among strategic units. Strategy choices impact MNC competitive advantage and organisational structure. The MNC competitive advantages are classified as location-based vs. system-based (Porter, 1990), with the latter being an important interface to link strategy with environment.

Porter pointed out that researchers in the past focused only on the key success factors of the MNCs, on the specific skills and secrets that MNCs obtained successfully in one country, and how MNCs could transfer these skills and secrets with low costs to other countries to offset the additional costs inherent in operating abroad. The scholars of strategic management, on the other hand, are more concerned about the management of the existing multinational companies and the strategic impact of international competition on MNCs. Thus, with the infusion of strategic perspective, the focus has shifted from existence to development mechanism, and has inspired a new understanding of the theoretical aspects of MNCs.

## Role of strategic alliances

International strategic alliance is an arrangement where two or more MNCs employ a cooperative approach to meet the entire global market targets, as well as their overall business objectives. With an explosion in various types of strategic alliances, MNCs are now perceived as alliance bodies consisting of a quasi-market with entangled relationships. Many scholars have analysed strategic alliances from various perspectives of transaction costs, technological innovation, competitive strategy and corporate structure. They all conclude that the development of MNC strategic alliances is a strategic response to the changes in international economy, technology and competitive environment. Strategic alliance is the product of changes in the global competitive environment.

The profound changes in the international competitive environment exerted tremendous pressure on MNC performance objectives. When multinational corporations analysed the competitive environment and evaluated their own competitive edge and resources, they often found a gap between the strategic performance goals expected by the competitive environment and the goal that they could achieve relying on their own resources and abilities. This gap is called the strategic gap. The strategic gap restricted MNCs who rely solely on their own resources and self-development. For this reason, strategic alliance became a rational choice for their growth. The strategic gap is an important motive that promotes strategic alliances in global competition. The larger the strategic gap for MNCs, the stronger the driving force to form strategic alliances.

Global strategic alliances or networks formed by firms and their associates from different countries constitute a long-term competitive advantage for MNCs. These alliances have had a noticeable impact on traditional MNC theory (Wu, 2000). Dunning (1993), for instance, expanded eclectic theory to analyse competitive advantages acquired from three sources: MNC operation process, increase in interdependence in intermediate markets and changes in resource distribution patterns among regions.

## The importance of strategic options

Myers (1977) and other scholars identified investments as equivalent to purchasing the right to exercise the option to exit or expand in the future. The present investment may get payback from the future investment options, and is the platform for future investment. In the early 1990s, Bowman and Hurry (1993) and Kogut and Kulatilaka (1994) applied the option theory to MNC strategy formulation. They concluded that MNCs may decide to defer investments to 'wait and see' until more information becomes available, and thereby enjoy additional benefits.

Rivoli and Salorio (1996) combined the strategic option theory and Dunning's eclectic theory to further explore the timing issues for MNC foreign investment. If foreign direct investment can be completely reversible, there is no reason for MNCs to postpone the foreign direct investment projects with positive net present value (NPV). The more powerful

25

the MNC's internal advantages, the more difficult it is for the MNC to exit after the investment and the greater the risk of the foreign direct investment being reversed. Therefore, strong internal advantages will increase the value of the option to delay foreign direct investment in an uncertain environment. Put another way, stronger internal advantages increase the possibility of using 'waiting' to replace immediate investment.

## MNC growth and development strategy theory

### International product life cycle theory

In 1966, Vernon, a Harvard Professor, published an article entitled 'International investments and international trade in the product cycle'. He used the product life cycle theory to explain the motives and development process of MNCs' investment strategy. Vernon constructed three stages of life cycle according to US MNCs' international growth process.

In the new product phase, the need is for great R&D skills, enormous investment for R&D and the high income and high consumption market conditions. Vernon believed that only the US has these conditions. Thus, in the innovative stage of product life cycle, new products are usually manufactured first in US innovative enterprises to reduce costs and acquire a monopoly on technology. Because US firms monopolised new technology, there was a lack of strong competitors. As a result, US firms controlled almost all the market shares. In the markets of other developed countries, consumers had to rely on the supply from US manufacturers because there were no domestic manufacturers.

In the second, mature product stage, new technology became more and more mature and so did product manufacturing. Although manufacturers could use the heterogeneity of new products to avoid direct price competition, efforts for cutting down production costs, transportation costs and tariffs became more important and demanding. For this reason, US MNCs started to invest and set up factories in other developed countries that used their products so that they could supply the market directly. This was imperative to maintain the existing market share and prevent potential competitors.

In the third standardised product stage, products were standardised with mass production. The innovative manufacturers no longer enjoyed the monopoly advantages. Competition was on price. At this time, resource conditions and cheap labour costs became increasingly decisive factors in the competitive edge of a product. The comparative advantages of production shifted to developing countries or regions with low levels of technology, low wages and labour-intensive economies. As a result, MNCs in developed countries started to invest directly in developing countries, transfer technology and reduce or halt their mass production in their native countries. They imported products from the developing countries to meet their local market needs.

MNC growth was attributed to changes over the course of the three-stage model. As new products experienced the new product stage, the maturity stage and the standardised stage, MNCs' choices of location for investments shifted from developed countries to more advanced developing countries and finally to less developing countries.

In 1974, Vernon published another article called 'The location of economic activities', which further advanced the product life cycle theory by introducing international monopoly behaviour to explain MNC direct overseas investment strategy. He defined all multinational corporations as monopolies and divided them into three categories – monopoly in technological innovation stage, monopoly in mature stage and monopoly in recession stage – corresponding with the three stages of the product life cycle.

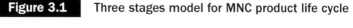

**Figure 3.1**  Three stages model for MNC product life cycle

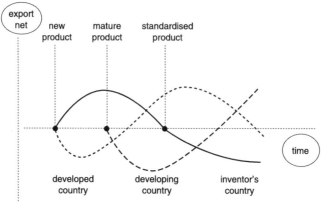

───── country where new product is launched
- - - - - other advanced, high-income country
– – – developing, low-income country

In the technological innovation stage, MNCs had the monopoly on manufacturing new products and enjoyed profits resulting from the monopoly. US MNCs used a domestic production base to innovate new products for timely, quick coordination among R&D, production and marketing activities. To maintain a monopoly, MNCs invested heavily in the financial and technical fields for product heterogeneity. For example, US MNCs invested in competitive advantages to meet the needs of high-income groups and in saving labour costs for innovative products and product heterogeneity. European MNCs invested in competitive advantages to save land resources and raw materials for product innovation and heterogeneity. When the product standardisation stage and foreign competitors emerged, US MNCs moved their production base abroad to a country with lower cost of production and transportation for supplying merchandise to overseas markets. Due to the different levels of economic development, MNCs use different skill levels and locations for foreign direct investment. For example, the majority of US MNCs chose to build manufacturing facilities in Western Europe or in Japan to make innovative new products. MNCs in Western European countries and Japan would normally choose to invest in countries and regions with even lower levels of economic development for their innovative new products.

In the maturity stage, there was imitation and dispersion of technology for producing innovative products and diminishing MNC technological advantages. Trade barriers in the local countries increased costs for importing innovative products into these countries. MNCs used foreign direct investment to maintain the monopolistic advantages for monopolistic profits. MNCs lost their monopoly advantages based on product innovation and the economy of scale became the basis of monopolistic advantages. MNCs changed their business strategies by making the best use of their multiple core competences in R&D, manufacturing and sales to raise entry barriers for their competitors. To acquire a greater share in their competitors' local market, MNCs invested directly in the major markets of their competitors to weaken the latter's competitive capabilities. Such direct foreign investments were accompanied by transfer of technology. Enterprises with a technological edge acquired monopolistic profits through proliferation of their technology. When an MNC took the lead in opening up a new market, other MNCs followed suit and adopted follow-up strategies to protect their positions in the international markets.

In the recession stage, MNCs lost their competitive advantages in both technology innovations and technology diffusion. This resulted in the gradual disappearance of profits. As a large number of standardised products flooded markets, price competition was particularly intense. Innovative enterprises made great efforts to reduce costs in order to make some profit. In this stage, MNCs lost their monopoly advantages even in economy of scale. Cost and price became the key to successful competition. Firms that were unable to cut down costs and prices were forced to withdraw from the market. Therefore, low cost of production became a major factor for MNC choice of foreign direct investment. Developing countries with cheap labour and huge market potential were optimal choices for MNC investment.

## MNC international direct capital withdrawal theory

International direct capital withdrawal is the antithesis of international direct investment. It means MNCs terminate all or part of their production activities in the host country or region. Taylor, Markides and Berg explained the various forms of investment withdrawal, with liquidation as the last resort. If there is no buyer for the existing production facility, liquidation occurs when the costs to close or sell the assets are lower than those to maintain the operation entities. Caves and Porter believed that if the investment revenue of a subsidiary continues to decline for some length of time and if the products of this subsidiary grow to maturity stage, divestment may occur – though the firms may be stopped from withdrawing because of various barriers to exit. Porter's studies on divestment obstacles and Wilson's classifications of international direct investment have had a great impact on the development of international direct divestment theories.

## MNC localisation theory

Before the 1970s, many developing countries perceived MNCs as greedy and cruel. MNCs invited strong criticism and opposition. With the changes in world politics and expanding global economy, developing countries are becoming more mature not only in politics but also in their economic conditions. To gain a foothold in developing countries, MNCs implemented new localisation strategies and made efforts to change their image. MNCs gradually established new relationships with the host countries. The so-called localisation efforts inspired MNCs to find partner firms in the local region and make contributions to the local business community. MNCs hired the host country's local talent for management positions and observed local traditional cultures thus creating transnational business models that adapted to the local business environment (Yang, 2000). The MNC localisation strategy included:

- market localisation strategy;
- personnel localisation strategy:
  - the parent company gradually gives local talent important management positions;
  - local enterprises process the operation time;
  - the steps for implementing personnel localisation strategy include: recruit outstanding students from host universities; participate in foreign talent recruitment activities by the host country; recruit employees using host intermediary services; establish research and development centres in the host country; set up employee training mechanisms in the host country;
- investment management localisation strategy;
- technology development localisation strategy;
- corporation culture localisation strategy;
- profit localisation strategy;
- material localisation strategy.

## Complex integration theory of MNC structure

Traditional MNC structure comprises independent subsidiaries. MNCs used ownership and technology provision to link the parent company with its subsidiaries. In a simple integration process, the relationship between MNC headquarters and foreign affiliates is loose. In a complex integration strategy, MNCs handle multiple connections and information communication between the parent company and its subsidiaries, among subsidiaries and among unrelated businesses. There is a tight relationship between MNCs' organisation management structure and the current stage of the internationalisation of production and operations.

MNCs have adapted to situational needs and adopted appropriate organisational structures for the needs of different stages of development: foreign trade, early direct investment, global production specialisation, regional investment decentralisation and globalisation of production and sales. The most typical examples are the parent–subsidiary structure, international structure, global structure and the multidimensional matrix management structure. When MNCs work in a low and loosely coordinated policy-making international mode, the parent–subsidiary structure or international structure is appropriate. But if an MNC needs high and tight international policy coordination, global organisation structure or matrix structure will be appropriate.

An appropriate choice of organisational structure can help MNCs implement their strategy, but the structure can also become an obstacle. For example, after a strategy change, the required structural change would normally not follow immediately. This is especially so when MNC managers get used to their roles within particular structures. From time to time, the demand for new structure tends to cause internal conflict, which will lead to long-term inefficiency. Obviously, the relationship between strategy and organisational structure is a complicated issue for any MNC. Therefore, in recent years, in the face of faster technological progress, MNCs have been seeking an innovative organisational structure to facilitate the implementation of MNC globalisation strategy.

## MNC parent–subsidiaries relationship evolution theory

Management of subsidiaries remains a challenge for MNCs. To implement the global strategic objectives of overall integration and network coordination, MNCs traditionally imposed their wishes on their subsidiaries. This practice limited the power and competence of subsidiaries and weakened their strategic independence, resulting in their stagnation. The system theory and cybernetics suggest that the MNC control of operational activities is a process of adjustment to maintain a stable operating system. Under the simple integration strategy, the evaluation of the subsidiary is based on firm growth and return on investment. Under the complex integration strategy, global companies focus on MNC overall performance rather than that of each subsidiary. Performance evaluation for subsidiary managers also includes their ability to complete the assigned tasks. Evaluation methods should address their responsibilities and the MNC should develop different appraisal systems accordingly.

As the MNC strategy evolves from simple functions and geographical links to more extensive, complex forms of integration, new trends are emerging.[3] For example, flexible production systems allow MNCs to make better use of small batch production, thus providing a physical barrier to withstand the pressure of global competition. Small batch production requires only a low level of integration and thereby reduces the minimum size of the market for profitable operations. This approach allows MNCs to adopt multiple local strategies. Since small and medium enterprises can effectively carry out small batch production, this approach,

**Table 3.1**    MNC strategy evolution and MNC structures

| Forms | Firm internal association | Degree of integration | Environmental conditions |
|---|---|---|---|
| Stand-alone subsidiaries (in multiple countries) | Proprietary and technology | Weak | Host country opens up for foreign direct investment with high trade barriers and high costs for communication and transportation |
| Simple integration (seeking external resources) | Proprietary, technology, market, bonuses and other inputs | Some are stronger and others are weak along the value chain | At least opening up bilateral trade and investment policy with non-equity arrangements |
| Complex integration (local core network) | All functions | The entire value chain has the potential in strengthening integration | Open trade and investment policies, advanced information technology with convergence of preferences and fierce competition |

in fact, works against the trend of integrated international production.

Table 3.1 summarises the three types of strategy that MNCs have adopted in the evolution process: stand-alone subsidiary, simple integration and complex integration. In the stand-alone subsidiary strategy, MNCs control and support many independent subsidiaries and each subsidiary provides independent service to each host country. In the simple integration or outsourcing strategy, MNCs use foreign partners for engaging in outsourced global production. Thus, some of the activities in the host country are moved to other countries and are linked primarily with the activities in the parent company. This indicates that the value-added activities have shifted to places or countries that are not the home or initial country, or the country for final sales. In the complex integration strategy, an MNC's global production can occur at any point in the value chain with the premise that it has the ability to transfer its production or supply capacity to any place in the world that can provide more profitability. MNC subsidiaries in any part of the world can perform the functions on their own or work together with the parent company or other subsidiaries. Complex integration requires that the various functions and activities can be arranged in the optimal places to conduct a comprehensive strategy to achieve the company's wishes.

## MNC diversification theory

Hood and Yang (1990) studied MNC diversification strategy in their book called Multinational Company Economics. They divided the diversification strategy into three types: horizontal strategy, vertical strategy and mixed expansion strategy. They discovered that US MNCs tend to favour horizontal diversification, while a considerable number of Japanese and British MNCs prefer vertical diversification. Japan's foreign investment strategy was a solution for those sectors with high labour costs, which led to a loss of comparative advantages at home. British MNCs originated from plantations and colonial companies in mining and ore extraction.

## *Distinctive features of the Japanese MNC strategy*

Early theoretical studies of MNCs were inspired by case studies of US MNCs. Professor Kojima of Hitotsubashi University in Japan published the book *On Foreign Direct Investment* in 1977. In his book, Kojima used the principle of international division of labour to construct a theory of comparative advantage to explain Japanese MNC foreign direct investment strategies. He believed that the US MNC strategy was based on micro factors, emphasising the impact of firm internal monopoly advantages on direct investment. The US firms engaging in direct investment had comparative advantages in the industrial manufacturing sectors. According to the principles of the international division of labour, the US should keep these manufacturing firms in the US and enjoy more benefits from expanding exports to other countries. However, these US firms competed with one another by investing in foreign manufacturing facilities and moved their production bases to foreign countries. The US exports were replaced by direct investments in foreign countries. As a result, the US trade conditions deteriorated because exports were greatly reduced and the international trade deficit greatly increased. Japan's foreign direct investment was different in that resource development accounted for major direct investments. Even in the manufacturing investment, Japan adopted trade manufacturing rather than a trade replacement policy. Firms that invested in foreign countries had comparative disadvantages in Japan's domestic production. Japanese firms moved their factories to the countries that enjoyed comparative advantage. Simply put, the foreign investment of Japan in manufacturing in fact spurred the exports of related products. This aligned the foreign direct investment with export trade to generate greater benefits for Japan (Kong, 2001).

Caimei Lin (1984) of Taiwan's Danjiang University identified the US MNC strategy in terms of the twin processes of product line expansion and geographical area expansion. These processes resulted in four stages: local-oriented enterprises (focus on expanding domestic geography), domestic-oriented enterprises (beginning with implementing product diversification in local market expansion and later in geographical expansion overseas), domestic-oriented enterprises overseas (product diversity, home market expansion and geographical expansion of the world market), and world-oriented enterprises (benchmark of product diversification and market expansion). As shown in Figures 3.2 and 3.3, traditionally, US MNCs focus on the domestic

**Figure 3.2**    History of US MNC development strategy

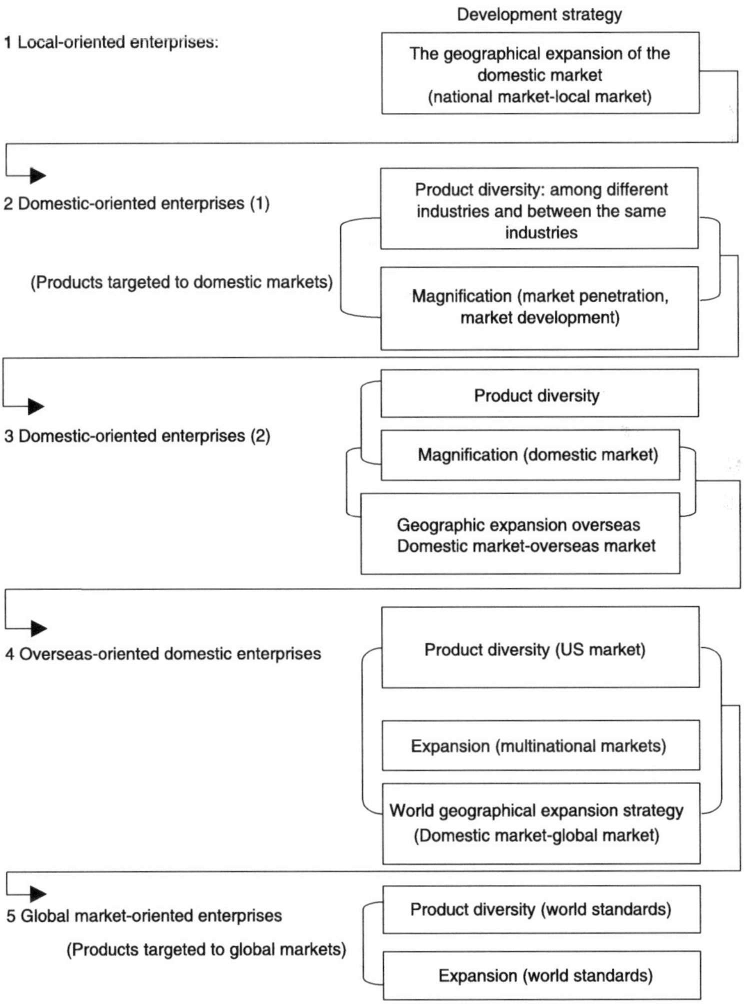

Development strategy

1 Local-oriented enterprises:

The geographical expansion of the domestic market
(national market-local market)

2 Domestic-oriented enterprises (1)

Product diversity: among different industries and between the same industries

(Products targeted to domestic markets)

Magnification (market penetration, market development)

3 Domestic-oriented enterprises (2)

Product diversity

Magnification (domestic market)

Geographic expansion overseas
Domestic market-overseas market

4 Overseas-oriented domestic enterprises

Product diversity (US market)

Expansion (multinational markets)

World geographical expansion strategy
(Domestic market-global market)

5 Global market-oriented enterprises

(Products targeted to global markets)

Product diversity (world standards)

Expansion (world standards)

**Figure 3.3** Model of US MNC development strategy

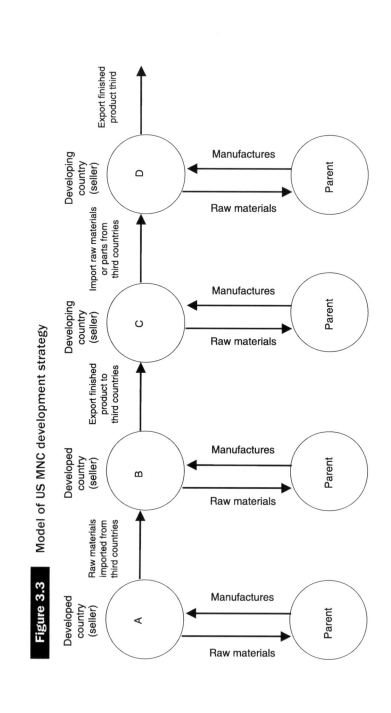

market for product diversification and leverage diverse products internationally through geographical diversification. They organise their operation based on international comparative advantage to benefit from the international division of labour. They use an integrated control policy to develop a product series and standardise different products in the series according to appropriate production advantage across different regions, such as the US, Europe and developing nations.

## Japanese multinational corporations' development strategies

Inspired by the work of Kansai University Professor Jianyi Jiangxia, Caimei Lin noted that Japanese MNCs strengthen comparative advantages in cost by not only focusing on production and labour costs, but also pursuing a balance between the domestic and the overseas market in order to learn, understand and incorporate technologies and techniques from other nations. They compete in advanced markets using sophisticated products made in Japan, and open up new international markets using simpler products made in third world nations. They also convert the product life cycle of technologies imported from advanced countries into a growth stage, through their transfer and direct investment in developing nations (see Figure 3.4).

Changsi Shijing[4] at the Zhuyou National Institute of Life in Japan gathered data from Japanese manufacturing enterprises that engaged in global businesses. Shijing summarised the expansion strategy of Japanese enterprises overseas into three stages: first, exports of domestic products and overseas sales; second, in order to adapt to the local market, a part of the production activities of the largely domestic products is in foreign countries; third, the domestic and overseas markets are unified from a global perspective

**Figure 3.4** Model of Japanese MNC development strategy

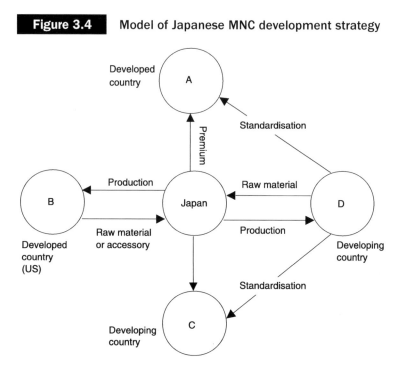

for research and development, purchase of materials and components, production, sales, finance and human resources. As the overseas operations are localised and offered more participation, Japanese MNCs focus on the company's strengths to successfully connect various overseas operations. They also seek to involve foreign enterprises in globalisation. The centre of technology development and production remains in Japan. An emphasis is put on a quick and accurate response to customers' requests through an information network of local product management to improve the relationship of production and marketing.

According to Shijing, Japanese MNC network globalisation is driven by the imperatives to manage the yen and tensions in the external environment. They develop a worldwide foundation base to select the best from the production base in the world, to produce accessories, products and low-priced software at the cheapest locations, and set up a common supply system to develop into a global network. They complement their globalisation strategy with a localisation strategy focused on acquiring business in host nations by providing employment opportunities. They adopt a quadruple system, where the world is divided into four areas: America, Europe, Asia and Japan (Asia along with Japan is sometimes referred to as the third pole). A fully integrated model is created for the maximised values coming from the advantages of these areas in their respective areas of product development, production, marketing, financial and other operational activities. The geographical omnibus company system transfers the firm-specific skills from local subsidiaries to a geographical omnibus headquarters, thereby helping to implement the strategy of maintaining a secure local contact.

It is worth noting that Shijing's analysis of the globalisation strategy of Japanese enterprises places the localisation strategy in a favourable position that is equivalent to globalisation. The perception of 'think globally, but act locally' is a significant foundation.

Professor Ming Shangye[5] at Shizuoka Prefecture University wrote the book *Sans Frontiers Time's Entrepreneurial Strategies* analysing the Japanese MNC competitive strategy in the Sans Frontiers time (globalisation time). 'Sans Frontières strategy' focuses on the overseas production across borders and exports from Japan as two channels to satisfy customer demand. Overseas production can cannibalise the domestic production for exports, if the two channels are not appropriately and organically linked. Japanese MNCs believe that products made in Japan are more appealing in the export target country; while products made overseas are in conflict with their global corporate image and trademark, and may even cause resentment among their customers. Therefore, products not produced locally in a nation must be imported from Japanese local businesses. As the capabilities of the local firms improve, the production by those firms will also be accepted by local clients. Thus, the expansion of overseas production does not obstruct the expansion of domestic exports; indeed, it helps to promote national exports.

According to Shangye, Japanese MNCs seek to place 'suitable products in the appropriate places' in order to achieve maximum efficiency and lowest cost for the corporate network, and appropriate benefits for various production bases. To ensure the success of subsidiaries within the international division of labour, Japanese MNCs emphasise the following conditions:

1. Overseas made products are manufactured at the same level of production quality and features as those produced domestically.

2. The overseas subsidiaries are expected to match the competitive advantages of Japan's domestic manufacturing industry in terms of the cost structures in order to maintain international competitiveness. Japanese MNCs therefore seek to transfer not only technology from domestic to overseas operations, but also the core competences in reducing costs and increasing labour productivity.

3. To fully engage overseas subsidiaries into their international division of labour as the global suppliers of parts and products, Japanese MNCs strive to build a very strong international marketing sales and global marketing network.

4. Japanese MNC headquarters play leading roles in external coordination and internal integration to cultivate the concept and understanding of the whole system, because the divisions cannot expand at the

expense of the corporate agenda. While the independent control of a production base for day-to-day operations is valued, the headquarters seek to maintain the authority for strategic activities including production models for various production bases, facility investment plans, production plans according to global need, and timing of products in global markets and total sales for various production bases worldwide and net profit expectations.

Japanese MNCs are showing commitment to sell back the products made in overseas subsidiaries into Japan, under their 'no frontier strategy'. 'No frontiers' refers to the highest form of international economic integration – while it has grown, it has not been achieved by Japanese MNCs. It is an adaptive business idea for the operations of Japanese enterprises in dealing with challenges from domestic and international business environments. It has the following features:

1. Increased imports help prevent trade tension and maintain the free trade system to bring maximum benefits to Japanese enterprises. The products sold back from overseas production are a favourable way to expand imports.

2. As the value of the Japanese yen has risen against the US dollar, production costs have been reduced in overseas enterprises, even when sold back to Japan.

3. With the transfer of better and more advanced technology and management knowledge from Japanese headquarters, overseas enterprises have been able to improve labour productivity and product quality, thereby meeting the expectations of domestic Japanese consumers.

4. Alongside the appreciation of the yen, per capita income and demand in Japan has continuously increased. Further, through an effective system of international division,

domestic and foreign production bases have developed their own features and competitive advantages. Consequently, the products produced overseas and sold back to domestic enterprises do not have a serious conflict and in fact result in increased sales of various products.

Philip Kottler,[6] a famous marketing professor at Northwestern University, has also examined the strategy of Japanese MNCs from the perspective of international marketing management. Accordingly to Kottler, the global market development strategy of Japanese MNCs comprises global market expansion and global marketing network development.

Global market expansion refers to the time sequence to access foreign target markets. Japanese firms expand into the global market in three time sequences:

1. Japan → developing countries → advanced countries. This is the main avenue through which Japanese firms entered the world market. For example, Japan's iron and steel, automobiles, petrochemicals, household appliances, clocks, camera equipment, pursued this route to enter the world market successfully. This process includes four stages: using the domestic market as a base for development; using developing countries as a springboard; targeting the US market; entering the European market.

2. Japan → advanced countries → developing countries. This category includes firms in such industries as computers, semiconductors and other high-tech industries of Japan. Due to the time lag in demand for high-tech products in developing countries, the firms in Japan first occupy the domestic market before they aim at the markets of the United States and other developed countries. Then the Japanese wait for opportunities for growth and demand from the developing countries.

3.  Advanced countries → Japan → developing countries. Although the majority of the overseas market for Japanese enterprises has followed the development of the first two examples, there are some exceptions. The original plans of certain products were aimed at developed countries outside of Japan, for example the video tape recorder and colour television. At that time, the demand for these products in Japan's domestic market was still quite weak. In 1964, colour TV in the United States was already very popular. In order to get more shares from the US market, firms in Japan made colour TVs in quantities and exported them to the US. Five years later, colour televisions became generally accepted in the Japanese domestic market.

Global marketing network development refers to the planning and layout of the marketing network throughout the entire world market. Japanese MNCs took more than 30 years to develop a strong and efficient global marketing network through six stages, thus ensuring the stability of their advantages in the global market:

1.  **Use commerce association as a springboard:** Most Japanese companies that were engaged in export businesses adopted this approach. Associations, especially comprehensive associations, were familiar with overseas markets. Through the portfolio of products and scale operations in different world regions, the comprehensive association could decentralise and absorb the price variances in the international market trade, thus lowering the risks of international exchange rates and tariffs. In addition, they provided a wide range of information on overseas markets, resulting in an efficient method for firm export services. The export service of

comprehensive association accounted for more than half of the businesses as the manufacturers' agents.

2. **Select and choose optimised partners:** After acquiring certain export sales experiences, some firms dismissed the commerce associations and located local distributors. Some Japanese businesses entered the US market through employing American manufacturers, which had superior sales channels and marketing capabilities.

3. **Establish Japanese overseas marketing companies:** Having got a foothold in the American market, many Japanese MNCs started to use their own distributing affiliates in the US to replace commerce associations and local dealers. In this way, they could use advertising, sales promotion and after-sales service to directly control and enhance marketing efforts and brand reputation in the target market.

4. **Set up plants and manufacture products in developing countries:** Towards the end of the 1960s, changes in the pattern of world politics and the economy had a far-reaching impact on Japanese companies. Under pressure from other countries in the world, Japan had to gradually open up its domestic market. With the appreciation of the yen, the Japanese currency, Japanese products lost their unique cost advantages. This spurred Japanese enterprises to seek new ways to maintain their competitive edge, particularly by setting up factories in developing countries to take advantage of the cheap labour and raw materials in production. Additionally, local production helped avoid the host country and third-country trade barriers.

5. **Local production in developed countries:** Direct investment in the United States and other developed countries helped Japanese MNCs cross the trade barrier

to consolidate their positions in the market. The growth or acquisition of self-invested factories of Japanese manufactures in the United States escalated.

6. **Gear to the global market:** In a global context, a firm with global orientation needs to make tough decisions such as these: in which part of the world to set up what kind of manufacturing plant; what kind of products to produce; which market to serve; and how to minimise the production and distribution costs. Many Japanese MNCs are using the principle of maximising the efficiency of their production to determine which functions should remain in the country and what arrangements should go abroad. They are evolving four internal division of labour systems in Japan, the United States, Europe and Asia.

# Evolution of MNC overseas subsidiaries strategy

The theoretical study of overseas subsidiaries of MNCs has a history of more than 20 years. During the 1970s, studies of overseas subsidiaries were sporadic, such as Youssef and Hulbert's preliminary study on overseas subsidiaries issues. In the early 1980s, Hedlund (1980) and Otterbeck (1981) studied autonomy and formalised organisation for MNC overseas subsidiaries. After these two studies, a large number of research studies on MNC overseas subsidiaries ensued. These studies covered areas such as relationships between the parent company and their subsidiaries, and the role and the development of MNC overseas subsidiaries. These studies have gradually become an important branch of theoretical studies on multinational corporations.

## Strategy–structure theory

Since the 1960s, inspired by Chandler's idea that structure follows strategy, many scholars tried to discover appropriate organisational structures based on the changes in MNC strategy. Strategy–structure study began as the stage model advocated by Stopford and Wells (1972). In 1989, Bartlett and Ghoshal proposed transnational organisation, which became the earliest branch of theoretical study on MNC overseas subsidiaries.

### International structure stage model

From a study of 187 of the largest multinational corporations in the United States in the late 1960s, Stopford and Wells (1972) suggested a stage model, a significant thread in the subsequent study of MNC subsidiaries. The stage model used the proportion of MNC foreign sales and the degree of product diversification as a yardstick in describing the evolutionary change process of MNC organisational structure in various stages of internationalisation. When foreign sales and product diversification were limited, the initial expansion abroad was structured through an international department. With the increased overseas expansion of foreign sales without significant increase in product diversity, MNCs usually employed a global regional structure. The MNCs that had increased sales through product diversity adopted the global products sector structure for their global expansion. Finally, when foreign sales and product diversity were both high, MNCs used the global matrix structure (Figure 3.5).

### Typology of structures for MNCs by Bartlett and Ghoshal

Bartlett and Ghoshal (1986) used the two-dimension research framework (globalisation pressure vs. local pressure) to

**Figure 3.5**  Stage model of Stopford and Wells (1972)

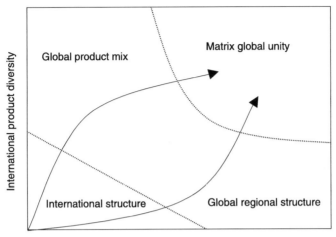

advance three types of MNC: global organisations, multinational organisations and transnational organisations. In 1989, Bartlett and Ghoshal further developed the three-quadrant model by Stopford and Wells (Figure 3.5) and replaced the original three-quadrant model with the four-quadrant model (Figure 3.6).

**Figure 3.6**  Bartlett and Ghoshal's (1989) chart of multinational organisations

**Figure 3.7**   Multinational organisation model

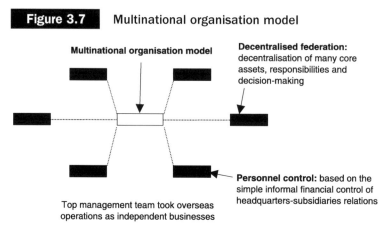

Multinational organisation model

**Decentralised federation:** decentralisation of many core assets, responsibilities and decision-making

**Personnel control:** based on the simple informal financial control of headquarters-subsidiaries relations

Top management team took overseas operations as independent businesses

Source: Bartlett and Ghoshal (2002). *Cross-border management*. (2nd edition). Translator: Yeging Ma, etc. Beijing. Demos Post and Telecommunications Publishing House.

The multinational organisation model is widely used by many European MNCs. In this model, the assets and management responsibilities are decentralised. The MNC maintains control over the subsidiaries using informal human coordination and the simple accounting system. The overseas operations are operated independently as decentralised federations (Figure 3.7).

The international organisation model is widely used for many American companies and is described as 'coordinated federation'. Assets and responsibilities are still scattered, but the subsidiaries are more dependent on the parent company's resources and under parent control. The parent company employs a formal management planning system for their subsidiaries and takes their overseas businesses as their affiliated units (Figure 3.8)

The global organisational model is widely used by many Japanese companies and is described as the 'centralised hub'. The resource, responsibilities and decision-making power are highly centralised in the parent company; subsidiaries serve only as sales units. There is a tighter control of the subsidiary by the parent company. Products and knowledge

**Figure 3.8**   International organisation model

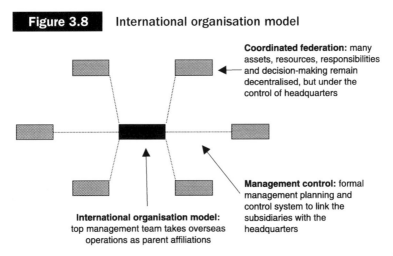

**Coordinated federation:** many assets, resources, responsibilities and decision-making remain decentralised, but under the control of headquarters

**Management control:** formal management planning and control system to link the subsidiaries with the headquarters

**International organisation model:** top management team takes overseas operations as parent affiliations

Source: Bartlett and Ghoshal (2002). *Cross-border management.* (2nd edition). Translator: Yeging Ma, etc. Beijing People's Post and Telecommunications Publishing House.

flow in one direction only. An overseas business is looked upon as the global market unification transmission channel (Figure 3.9).

A multinational organisation is highly sensitive and has a rapid response for the difference between markets and political demands of different countries. International organisations

**Figure 3.9**   Global organisation model

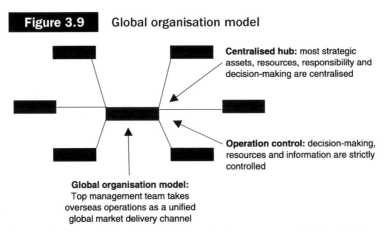

**Centralised hub:** most strategic assets, resources, responsibility and decision-making are centralised

**Operation control:** decision-making, resources and information are strictly controlled

**Global organisation model:** Top management team takes overseas operations as a unified global market delivery channel

Source: Bartlett and Ghoshal (2002). *Cross-border management.* (2nd edition). Translator: Yeging Ma, etc. Beijing People's Post and Telecommunications Publishing House.

**Figure 3.10** Transnational organisation models

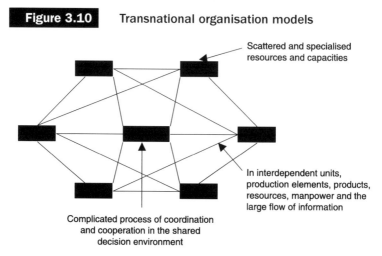

Scattered and specialised resources and capacities

In interdependent units, production elements, products, resources, manpower and the large flow of information

Complicated process of coordination and cooperation in the shared decision environment

Source: Bartlett and Ghoshal (2002). *Cross-border management*. (2nd edition). Translator: Yeging Ma, etc. Beijing People's Post and Telecommunications Publishing House.

offer an effective track for transferring knowledge from a parent company in accordance with local needs as required. Global organisations promote the development of coordinated strategies to achieve global economies of scale and efficiency. However, none of these alone can accomplish the integrative strategic capabilities that each structure can offer. Hence, there is a need for a new learning structure or model that can distribute strategic assets for both decentralisation and specialisation that support different organisational roles and diversification. Transnational organisations were designed for such a purpose. In these, the assets and resources are scattered and the role and responsibilities of the subsidiaries are varied. A variety of innovative ways of sharing global knowledge are deployed (Figure 3.10).

Table 3.2 summarises the comparison of the four MNC organisation models.

As the father of theoretical studies of MNC overseas subsidiaries, the strategy and structure school has not only explained a number of issues in global operations but also provided an effective way to understand the differences in

**Table 3.2** Comparison of four MNC organisational models

| Organisation characteristics | Organisation model | | | |
|---|---|---|---|---|
| | Multinational organisation | Global organisation | International organisation | Transnational organisation |
| Allocation of assets and capabilities | Scattered, national self-sufficiency | Focus, global scale | Ability to focus on core source; others scattered | Scattered, interdependent assets and resources |
| Role of overseas business | Find and make use of opportunities | Implement the strategy of the parent company | Adjust and use the parent company's ability | The difference in subsidiary's role; specialisation |
| Development and proliferation of knowledge | Units develop and maintain their own knowledge | Central development and possession of knowledge | Central development in knowledge and transfer to overseas units | Develop and share knowledge around the world |
| Form | Scattered union | Centralisation centre | Collaboration alliance | Integrated network |
| Strategic capability | Local response | Global efficiency | Global innovation and learning | Balance among local response, global efficiency and global learning |

MNC performance. Stronger performance is a function of the appropriate alignment between corporate strategy and environmental needs and the match between strategies and organisational structures.

However, there are many flaws of the strategy–structure school. Since the 1980s, the international competition environment has become increasingly complex, with both global integration pressure and local responsiveness pressure. In theory, the matrix structure can take care of the pressures from the two aspects at the same time, but thanks to its dual-control mechanism, the decision-making progress is lengthy and slow. The conflict from the dual leadership may ultimately lead to a strategic failure. Indeed, Bartlett (1983) reported that the MNCs which adopted the matrix structure did not enjoy more outstanding performance than those with a simple international structure. Moreover, the strategy–structure school takes the entire MNC as a unit of analysis and focuses on the overall differences among multinational corporations – rather than on the roles of the MNC overseas subsidiaries.

## Parent–subsidiaries relationship school

During the 1980s, scholars began to shift attention from the overall structure to the internal relationships within MNCs. The parent–subsidiaries school focuses on the vertical relationship between the parent company and the subsidiaries, emphasising how the parent company effectively controls and coordinates its overseas subsidiaries.

### Prahalad and Doz's study

Prahalad and Doz pointed out in their 1987 study that the control of the parent company over subsidiaries was the core of the relationship between a parent company and subsidiaries, and studied the control model and tools.

Factors that enhance the control ability of the parent company include:

1. The dependence of subsidiaries on the parent company's resources (e.g. technology, markets, financial or management resources) can help improve the control of the parent company over the subsidiaries. The dependence occurs when none of the affiliates has adequate skills or resources to replace all the functions of the parent company. The subsidiaries cannot survive in isolation from other entities of the group, no matter how big they are, how mature their technology is nor how complex the operations they can manage. In addition, if subsidiaries have to depend on the parent company for technical or management resources, the parent company is able to use this dependence to influence its subsidiaries' behaviour.

2. If subsidiaries hold a common strategic intent and competitive strategies with the parent company, it is more conducive to the control of the parent company.

3. If subsidiaries' contributions are measured against the global network rather than the performance in the local

| Table 3.3 | Control of the parent company over subsidiaries' operations |
|---|---|

| Factor strengthening the control ability | Factor weakening the control ability |
|---|---|
| Dependence of subsidiaries on the parent company's resources: technology, management, export markets, finance | Subsidiaries' degree of autonomy: evolution of relationship between the parent company and subsidiaries |
| Shared strategic perception and competitive strategies | The host government control |
| Evaluation system for contribution to global strategy | Existence of joint venture partners |
| Loyalty to the parent firm | Loyalty to the host country |

Source: Prahalad and Doz (2001). *The multinational mission*. Translator: Wenbin Wang, etc. Beijing: Huaxia Publishing House.

market, it is more beneficial to the control of the parent company.

4. The more loyal the subsidiaries to the parent company and the higher their sense of commitment, the easier the control of the parent company.

Factors that hinder the control ability of the parent company include:

1. **Evolution of the subsidiaries:** with the development of their own resources and abilities, subsidiaries gradually reduce their dependence on the parent company.

2. **Host government control:** if the host government exerts strong strategic influence in its territory over the subsidiaries, the coordination and control of the parent company becomes difficult.

3. **Influence of joint venture partners:** as the motive of subsidiaries operating with local joint-venture partners may not be consistent with the parent company's motives, the control of the parent companies becomes difficult.

4. **The degree of loyalty of subsidiaries to the host country:** the more loyal the subsidiaries and stronger the sense of belonging to the host country, the more difficult is the control of the parent company.

Doz and Prahalad identified three types of control tool (Table 3.4):

- **Data management tools:** databases that can be used for both key strategic decisions as well as global and local operations aid conversion of the raw data into useful information to expedite decision-making and strategic control.

- **Managers' incentive tool:** rules of the game enable managers to shape their understanding of their own

| Table 3.4 | Control tools |

| Data management tool | Manager incentive tool | Conflict management tool |
|---|---|---|
| 1 Information system | 1 Key managers' choices | 1 Allocation of decision-making responsibilities |
| 2 Evaluation system | 2 Promotion channels | 2 Comprehensive balance staff |
| 3 Resource allocation procedures | 3 Reward and punishment system | 3 Business groups |
| 4 Strategic plan | 4 Career development | 4 Coordination committee |
| 5 Budget plan | 5 Socialisation model | 5 Taskforce |
| | | 6 Problem-solving procedures |

Source: Prahalad and Doz (2001). *The multinational mission*. Translator: Wenbin Wang. Beijing: Huaxia Publishing House.

benefits and expectations. The appointment and promotion procedures, personal assessment, reward and punishment, and career development planning are all the rules of the game conducive to a large number of senior and middle-level managers.

■ **Conflict management tools:** this tool provides a channel or framework for solutions to the disputed issues, especially for balancing the issue of globalisation and regional response.

## Ghoshal and Nohria's study

Ghoshal and Nohria showed in a study in 1989 that the parent company should adopt different modes of management control and coordination under varying structural situations.

Ghoshal and Nohria defined a typology of four structural situations using two dimensions: environmental complexity and resource level. Environmental complexity includes such

**Figure 3.11**  Control and coordinated model of Ghoshal and Nohria

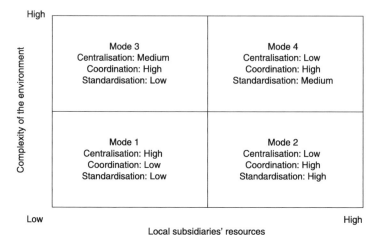

Source: Xi Youmin (2002).

host country factors as market, political, legal, regulatory, cultural and social, and natural and geographical forces. Resource level includes a subsidiary's accumulated knowledge, experiences and capabilities in the process of local production. In accordance with the different situations of MNC subsidiaries, the parent company should adopt three different control and coordinated modes to manage and control their subsidiaries (Figure 3.11).

Ghoshal and Nohria also identified three control and coordinated methods:

- **centralised management:** a formal authority and hierarchical system of decision-making processes, where the subsidiaries lack autonomy in choices;
- **standardised control:** decision-making through administrative mechanisms such as systematic rules and procedures;
- **regulating coordination:** the managers together with the followers have a set of shared goals, values and beliefs for guiding their concepts and behaviours.

## Martinez and Jarillo's study

Martinez and Jarillo (1989) divided the control mechanisms into two types: formal control mechanisms and informal control mechanisms. Formal control mechanisms include a formal organisational structure, the distribution of decision-making power, standardised procedures, the budget plan, and the results and the control of behaviour as the major structure. Informal control mechanisms include cross-functional linkages, informal communication and the corporate culture with value assimilation as the major structure (Table 3.5).

**Table 3.5**    Classification of control mechanism

| Type | Form | Description |
|---|---|---|
| Formal mechanism | Formal organisational structure | The organisation structure forms through division of labour and departments |
| | Allocation of decision-making power | Distribution of decision-making power in different levels of chain of command |
| | Formalisation and standardisation | Policy, rules and procedures in the organisational document system |
| | Plan | System and process such as strategic plan and budget |
| | Results and behaviour control | Control based on documents submitted to the management, reporting and minutes; direct monitoring of behaviours |
| Informal mechanism | Cross-function departments, communications | Direct contacts among managers of different departments, working groups, committees and teams |
| | Informal communication | Informal contacts among managers of different departments, managers' visit and work transfers |
| | Corporate culture | Assimilation process through personal understanding of organisational behaviours, decision-making process, goals and values |

Source: Xi Youmin (2002).

**59**

The study of the control mechanism of MNCs emphasised a gradual transition between the 1920s and the 2000s from formal to informal control mechanisms. This, Martinez and Jarillo explained, was due to the rapid changes in the global business environment and competition rules. As the MNCs changed their business strategy, they needed to change organisational structure and control mechanisms also (see Table 3.6).

## Bartlett and Ghoshal's study

Bartlett and Ghoshal pointed out in 1989 that the management tradition of MNCs impacts the method of coordination of the parent company over their subsidiaries. The MNCs in Japan, the United States and Europe tend to use three different coordination approaches.[7]

**Centralisation** is the dominant approach for Japanese MNCs. The parent company issues direct commands and makes independent decisions for the subsidiaries. In Japanese corporate culture, decisions require the views and inputs from the majority of members for a thorough communication. The decision-making process takes a long time and is very slow. Centralised coordination helps make more rapid decisions to minimise the friction between the parent company and subsidiaries from fragmentation of power. However, the parent company often finds it difficult to respond quickly to local needs when the host environment changes rapidly.

**Formalisation** is the dominant approach for US MNCs. The parent company deploys formal systems, policies and standards to manage subsidiaries. The management power of both the parent company and its overseas subsidiaries is reduced through an independent and objective policy, thereby resulting in standardisation and efficiency. However,

**Table 3.6** Evolution of control mechanisms

| Time period | MNC organisational structure | Main control mechanism |
|---|---|---|
| Period 1 1920–1950 multinational phase | Decentralised federal: A high degree of autonomy from the overseas subsidiaries forms loose alliances; each subsidiary is concerned only about its own local market | Formal control mechanisms:<br>■ international structure;<br>■ direct personal report;<br>■ rarely rely on the results control, but use financial performance;<br>■ send personnel from the parent company to implement behaviour control |
| Period 2 1950–1980 global phase | Centralisation centre: Provide value activities for firm competitive advantages (generally upstream activities, such as product design or manufacture) concentrated in the parent company or strictly controlled by the parent company | Formal control mechanisms:<br>■ regional, international or global structure;<br>■ the parent company is highly centralised in decision-making;<br>■ high degree of standardisation for policies, rules and process;<br>■ standardisation for planning and budgeting system |
| Period 3 1980–2010 transnational phases | Integrated network: Assets and the ability scattered in overseas subsidiaries to form an integrated network of scattered resources but interdependent subsidiaries; each subsidiary is a source of resources | Formal control mechanisms:<br>■ global matrix structure;<br>■ centralised decision-making, but strengthen subsidiaries' functions;<br>■ high degree of standardisation;<br>■ rely on strategic plan;<br>■ tight and complicated results control.<br>Informal control mechanisms:<br>■ teamwork, working group, committee and general staff;<br>■ informal channels of communication and contact among managers;<br>■ build strong organisational culture through shared values and goals |

Source: Xi Youmin (2002).

the MNC has to incur high costs to make any adjustments if the current system and procedures cannot fit environmental changes. In addition, in an environment shaped by routine-driven standardisation, managers' initiatives for innovation are seriously suppressed.

**Socialisation** is the dominant approach for European MNCs, who use the parent company's corporate culture and management philosophy to manage their subsidiaries. Since the social model depends on common values and goals, it represents a more dynamic and flexible system of coordination. However, the biggest challenge in the social model is the high operating costs, for example, costs incurred in training the entire management team and instilling culture values in them.

## *MNC subsidiary role school*

Many scholars have tried to identify the roles of overseas subsidiaries using different perspectives (Bartlett and Ghoshal, 1986; Jarillo and Martinez, 1990; Gupta and Govindarajan, 1991; Taggart, 1996). As each of the subsidiaries is established by the MNCs, they all have a specific strategic task in the MNC network.

### White and Poynter's classification theory

White and Poynter (1984) identified five categories of the roles of MNC overseas subsidiaries using three aspects: (1) product scope: flexibility in product policy to increase the production line and expand facilities; (2) market scope: the geographical range between the local market and the global market; and (3) value-added areas: the rate of value realised through activities in development, manufacturing and/or marketing.

1. **Micro copy of parent company:** this type of overseas
   subsidiary is a microcosm of the parent company to
   produce and/or sell selected products in the parent
   company's chain of products. MNCs adopt this approach
   when they suffer from many constraining factors, including
   local preference (such as food), trade barriers, local
   manufacturing subsidy, low degree of economies of scale
   in production or higher transportation costs. These factors
   force subsidiaries to copy their parent company and make
   it impossible for them to use an integrated production
   strategy. Subsidiary miniature replicas are sub-classified
   into three types: (1) exact copy: the product and marketing
   plan come from the parent company and is introduced to
   the local market without any changes; (2) modified copy:
   the product and marketing plan are changed to meet the
   local market needs and preferences, subject to a cost
   analysis of this adaptation; (3) reformed copy: to avoid
   excess capacity and to take the best use of the local
   distribution network to develop related new products, the
   tenure of operations is important in selecting a subsidiary's
   strategies. For example, the newly established overseas
   subsidiaries are often discouraged to become a reformer
   or mini-replicas. MNC overseas subsidiaries usually need
   to go through a natural development process, which starts
   with an exact copy model and gradually evolves into
   development of its featured strategy.

2. **Sales satellite:** this role works well for overseas
   subsidiaries that are not involved in manufacturing and
   are only responsible for selling products made by the
   parent company or other subsidiaries. Occasionally they
   are engaged in simple packaging or processing operations.
   This type of overseas subsidiary might be a single
   company that functions as wholesaler or could be a
   vendor who has a broad distribution. The feature of this

strategy is to service the local market while the scope of value is small. The strategy is practical for firms using low-cost strategy or global differentiation strategy.

3. **Rational manufacturer:** this type of overseas subsidiary produces parts or finished products for a multi-country market or global market. If it produces parts of a product, the product will be exported to other units of the multinational corporation for further processing. There is a limited range for products and value-added scope. Sales for the finished products are mainly done by the sales satellite subsidiaries of the MNC. Research and development are conducted inside the MNC. The parent company also retains the decision-making power in such areas as the creation and expansion of the variety of products and increase in production capacity. This type of model works better when the economies of scale and geographic factors become favourable for mass production to serve several markets. For example, in the semiconductor industry most parts are manufactured in one subsidiary to supply the products to other MNC units for assembly.

4. **Product experts:** these subsidiaries develop, produce and sell a limited range of products for a multi-country or global market and enjoy freedom in aspects of R&D, manufacturing and sales. Of course, subsidiaries need to have good communication so that the parent company can implement strategic control of these recognised products. The parent company grants the product expert subsidiaries the authority to operate independently in developing, manufacturing and selling their new products in regional or global markets.

5. **Strategic independence:** these overseas subsidiaries have their own resources and can provide new lines of products

to a local market, a multi-country market or global market. The parent company does not restrict their access to the global market; nor does it restrict these subsidiaries to develop new businesses. This type of subsidiary bears features similar to capital investors. However, it keeps close ties with its parent company in structure and finance. There are only a small number of such strategic independent overseas subsidiaries.

## Bartlett and Ghoshal's theory

Bartlett and Ghoshal (1989) believed that the strategic position of overseas subsidiaries is not only determined by the organisational form of the parent company but also by the capabilities of overseas subsidiaries and the market resources they have. A subsidiary's strategic position depends largely on how important its host environment is to the MNC global strategies.[8] They classified four types of tasks of the overseas subsidiaries (Figure 3.12).

**Figure 3.12**  Bartlett and Ghoshal's classification of strategic task model

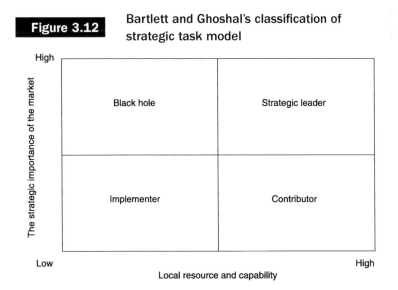

1. **Strategic leader:** overseas subsidiaries cooperate with the parent company to implement the strategy of the MNC. However, only those overseas subsidiaries that have strong competitive advantages in the market are in a strategic position to accomplish this task.

2. **Contributor:** the overseas subsidiaries that undertake this task are located in a market of a smaller scale or of insignificant strategic position. However, these subsidiaries have resources and competitive strengths and thus they are important to the parent company.

3. **Local implementer:** overseas subsidiaries doing this task have the ability to maintain local businesses, but usually operate in an insignificant market. It is difficult for these overseas subsidiaries to get important information because resources are limited and they do not have the conditions to become contributors or provide strategic leadership. However, the roles of these firms are significant because they help add values to the MNC and provide funds for the MNC's routine operations and future development.

4. **Black hole:** in a larger market that has an important strategic position, the market shares and competitive edge of MNC overseas subsidiaries tend to be insignificant and thus a market of this nature is described as a black hole. MNCs must be able to manage in this environment so that their subsidiaries can gradually phase into the other three positions. MNCs wanting to establish powerful local control face intense competition in the host environment and find it both time- and cost-consuming. For this reason, many Korean and Taiwan computer manufacturers set up a small subsidiary in the black hole, such as in the American Silicon Valley, as a 'window' to observe American technology. Many MNCs from the US and Europe made similar efforts of building a small

subsidiary in Japan to gather information and surveillance Japan's technological development for their headquarters so as to make a pre-emptive attack in dealing with their competitors and sustain their competitive advantages in the global market. To serve as a keen observation window for technology development, these subsidiaries must be very sharp and sensitive to any strategic changes to take action before their competitors.

## Dunning's theory

In 1988, Dunning proposed the motive of property right as the decisive factor for overseas subsidiaries' economic activities, business scope and strategic position in MNCs. Using the property motivation theory, Dunning classified the MNC overseas subsidiaries into:

1. market-expanding subsidiaries, seeking to overcome trade barriers to protect the MNC's export markets;

2. resource-expanding subsidiaries, seeking to obtain natural resources, cheap labour and other low-cost production essentials;

3. efficiency-expanding subsidiaries, which are professional production enterprises;

4. strategic asset-expanding subsidiaries, which are a more recent development as a result of mergers and acquisitions (M&As). M&As not only transfer skills and abilities of MNCs to their subsidiaries, but also protect and make the best use of the skills and capabilities of the acquired subsidiaries to enhance the overall MNC competitiveness.

## Jarillo and Martinez's theory

In 1990, Jarillo and Martinez used Prahalad and Doz's I-R framework, based on two dimensions – the degree of

**Figure 3.13**    Jarillo and Martinez's model of subsidiary roles

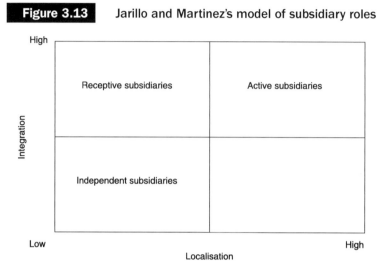

localisation in business activities and the degree of integration in operational activities – to define three types of overseas subsidiary (Figure 3.13):

- **Independent subsidiaries** are independent of the parent company and other subsidiaries and engage in most of the value-chain activities and across multiple local industries.

- **Receptive subsidiaries** engage in only a few business activities, such as marketing, sales or simple manufacturing or mining, while working closely with other MNC subsidiaries. They are common among centralised MNCs.

- **Active subsidiaries** engage in a variety of business activities and work closely with other MNC activities. They enjoy high autonomy and maintain a close relationship with the parent company.

## Gupta and Govindarajan's theory

Gupta and Govindarajan (1991) used two dimensions – the degree of knowledge flow and the direction of knowledge

**Figure 3.14**   Role of node in knowledge flow

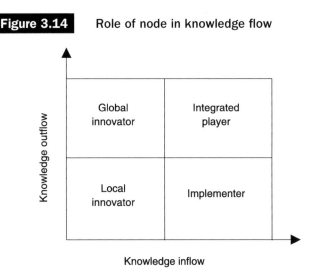

Source: Gupta and Govindarajan (1991).

flow – to construct four nodes in an MNC network (Figure 3.14):

- **Global innovator** has low knowledge inflow and high knowledge outflow – it plays a major role in providing knowledge to other subsidiaries in the MNC network. Historically, especially in MNCs from the US and Japan, only the parent company played this role. However, increasingly the global innovator may be an overseas subsidiary. For example, in the Swedish MNC Ericsson, the Italian subsidiary serves as the research centre for transmission systems and the Finnish subsidiary for mobile communications.

- **Integrated player** also has high knowledge inflow and high knowledge outflow – it also supports other nodes of the MNC network and plays an important role in creating and transmitting knowledge. However, instead of creating all the knowledge, it relies more on other nodes in the network for knowledge flow. It assimilates knowledge and creates new knowledge based on the absorption of the knowledge from other nodes and in turn transmits the knowledge back to other nodes in the network. The Japanese subsidiary of IBM is a case in point.

- **Implementer** has high knowledge inflow and low knowledge outflow – it has hardly any knowledge-innovative activities of its own but relies on the parent company and other subsidiaries in the network for knowledge inflows. Historically, most overseas subsidiaries operated as the implementer and obtained the knowledge and technology from the parent MNC. The subsidiaries of the 3M Corporation in small countries such as Finland are examples.

- **Local innovator** has low knowledge inflow and low knowledge outflow – it relies on its own local resources for innovating knowledge and skills that are needed for all its functional areas. It seldom depends on other nodes in the network for its knowledge inflow and sends little knowledge to other nodes. Traditional multi-domestic MNCs were composed of subsidiaries that were in fact local innovators. For example, at the Kentucky Fried Chicken (KFC) subsidiaries in Japan, the architectural style, restaurant size, theme and menu choices are very different from other subsidiaries that imitated those from the headquarters in the US.

## Taggart's theory

In 1996, Taggart applied Porter's 'coordination–allocation' framework to construct the C–C (coordination–configuration) strategy model for MNC overseas subsidiaries. The model consists of four types of strategy (Figure 3.15):

- **Confederate subsidiaries** correspond to high decision-making autonomy, alongside extensive management coordination.

**Figure 3.15**     Taggart's C–C subsidiaries strategy model

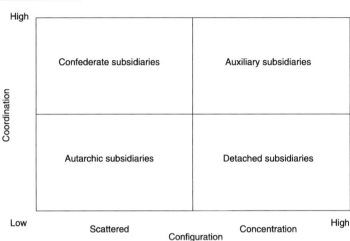

- **Auxiliary subsidiaries** correspond to a global strategy and operate under high management coordination, lacking decision-making autonomy. However, they have access to higher technical skills from the parent MNC, which facilitates access to international markets.

- **Autarchic subsidiaries** correspond to a country-centred strategy – the configuration of value chain activities is scattered across subsidiaries with significant decision-making autonomy. Each subsidiary has low management coordination and integration with the parent company.

- **Detached subsidiaries** correspond to an export-based strategy – the configuration of value chain activities is concentrated in the home region of the parent company. The subsidiaries have low management coordination and integration with the parent company, and low decision-making autonomy.

Table 3.7 summarises the findings from various studies related to subsidiary roles. In summary, the school of scholars on the role of subsidiaries recognised that different subsidiaries possess different roles in the global strategy of MNCs. These scholars argued for making the subsidiaries' role the main focus in MNC research and took the parent company as the external variable. They recognised the internal differences and diversity of the MNC networks and shifted the focus of study from taking the MNCs as a whole to the roles of subsidiaries. However, these scholars studied and analysed the status and roles of the MNC overseas subsidiaries from a static analysis perspective. Once the roles were identified for the subsidiaries, there was no continued research into change and development. Thus we do not see any in-depth studies on long-term progress and the role evolution path for these MNC subsidiaries.

## Subsidiaries' development school

The research on subsidiaries' development focuses on the dynamic nature of how the roles and positions of overseas subsidiaries are constantly evolving over time. During the 1980s, in the process of studying the relationship between the parent company and its subsidiaries and subsidiary roles, some scholars started investigating MNC overseas strategy evolution from a development perspective (Prahalad and Doz, 1981; White and Poynter, 1984; Jarillo and Martinez, 1990). In recent years, as the global business environment has experienced rapid change, the development perspective has become an important branch of MNC research.

In 1998, Birkinshaw and Hood summarised the general patterns and influencing factors on subsidiary evolution.[9] Birkinshaw believed that the process of overseas subsidiary evolution was closely related to two concepts: capabilities and charter.

**Capabilities** are abilities of MNC subsidiaries to achieve the desired objectives and goals via an organising process to

**Table 3.7** Summary of studies on subsidiary roles

| Author | Empirical/ conceptual | Research focus | Sample | Variable | Low integration | | High integration | |
|---|---|---|---|---|---|---|---|---|
| | | | | | Low/low | High/low | Low/high | High/high |
| White and Poynter (1984) | Conceptual | Subsidiaries | 36 subsidiaries managers | Product range; Market range; Added value range; Market range; | Micro-copy (adaptor); Sales satellite | Micro-copy (innovator) | Product experts; Rationalised manufacturer | Independent strategy |
| Porter (1986) | Conceptual | Overall company | | Coordinate; Distribution | | Country strategy | Global strategy | Complex global strategy |
| Bartlett and Ghoshal (1986) | Empirical | Specific subsidiaries | 518 subsidiaries | Ability; Importance of strategy | Black hole | Local implementer | Contributor | Strategic leader |
| Prahalad and Doz (1987) | Empirical | Overall company | More than 20 firms from Europe, US and Japan | Integration and response | | Local reaction strategy, Independent national subsidiaries | Integrated product strategy, Global business management | Multinational strategy; Matrix organisation |
| Bartlett and Ghoshal (1989) | Empirical literature reviews | Overall company | 3 European firms, 3 Japanese firms and 3 US firms | Adaptability Coordination cross-national application ability | MNCs | International organisation | Global organisation | Transnational organisation |
| Jarillo and Martinez (1990) | Empirical | Specific subsidiaries | 50 Spanish subsidiaries | Local integration | | Receptive subsidiaries | Independent subsidiaries | Active subsidiaries |

(continued)

**Table 3.7** Summary of studies on subsidiary roles (*continued*)

| Author | Empirical/ conceptual | Research focus | Sample | Variable | Low integration | | High integration | |
|---|---|---|---|---|---|---|---|---|
| | | | | | Low/low | High/low | Low/high | High/high |
| Gupta and Govindarajan (1991) | Conceptual | Subsidiaries | | Knowledge outflow; Knowledge inflow | Low outflow, low inflow; Local innovator | High inflow, low outflow; Implementer | Low inflow, high outflow Global innovator | High inflow; high outflow; Integration |
| Birkinshaw and Morrison (1995) | Empirical | Subsidiaries | 50 Spanish subsidiaries | Autonomy; Integration activities | | Local implementer | Specialised contributor | Entrusted worldwide |
| Taggart (1997) | Empirical | Specific subsidiaries | 171 UK subsidiaries | Coordination; Distribution | Silent type subsidiaries | Receptive subsidiaries | Independent subsidiaries | Active subsidiaries |
| Surlemont (1998) | Empirical | Subsidiaries | 662 relative units | Power; Capacity | Dormancy centre | Superior strategic centre | Management centre | Global headquarters |
| Randoy and Li (1998) | Empirical | Subsidiaries | US subsidiaries of 25 industries | Resource inflow; Resource outflow | Independent resource | Resource users | Global resources provider | Resource network workers |
| Taggart (1998) | Empirical | Specific subsidiaries | 171 foreign firms in UK | Coordination; Distribution | Dictatorship subsidiaries | Subsidiaries | Federal strategy | Strategic support |
| Taggart (1999) | Empirical | Specific subsidiaries | 265 manufacturing subsidiaries in UK | Autonomy Procedure approval | Militants | Local leaders | Partnership | Cooperative relations |
| Solberg (2000) | Conceptual | Overall company | | Market knowledge; Autonomy | Civil way | Local leaders | Alliance | Federal |

utilise and integrate resources. Because each subsidiary has its own unique growth route and geographical location, the capability of each subsidiary is different from those of the parent company and other overseas subsidiaries. Subsidiary capabilities are accumulated in the course of its growth and have path dependency – making it hard to transfer and spread the capabilities to other subsidiaries.

**Charter** is the subsidiary's functions and responsibilities granted by the parent. The scope of charter is very wide and may include market service, products, technology, functional areas or any combination. In most MNCs, through internal competition, one subsidiary may obtain the charter of another subsidiary. In some cases, two subsidiaries may compete with each other for a new charter.

Capability is the foundation for the status and roles of subsidiaries and is recessive, while charter is the external exhibition of subsidiary roles and functions and is the overt part. The evolution of subsidiaries is an interactive process of increase or decrease of subsidiary capabilities and of gains or losses of charter.

Using the two dimensions of change of capabilities and change of charter, Birkinshaw proposed the evolution model of MNC overseas subsidiaries. Each dimension includes three levels: recession, consolidation and increase. He thus identified five patterns, as shown in Figure 3.16:

- **Pattern 1:** parent-driven investment (PDI) is the subsidiary capacity increase thanks to the parent company charter grant. To increase investment in a project, the parent company conducts a comparative evaluation of subsidiaries at different locations and grants a charter to one suitable subsidiary. Having obtained the new charter, the capacity of this subsidiary is enhanced in the process of charter implementation.

| Figure 3.16 | Evolution models of overseas subsidiaries |
|---|---|

Source: Birkinshaw and Hood (1998b).

- **Pattern 2:** subsidiary-driven charter extension (SDE) is the gain of charters from the parent company thanks to capability increase of the subsidiaries. In their growth process, MNC subsidiaries use their entrepreneurial spirit and proactive initiative in seeking and utilising new business opportunities and enhance their capabilities in the process of long-term efforts. When the parent company recognises their potential, the subsidiaries are granted more charters.

- **Pattern 3:** subsidiary-driven charter reinforcement (SDR) is the subsidiary capacity consolidation that helps consolidate the existing charter. In the continuous competitive process with other subsidiaries and with external competitors, subsidiaries consolidate their capabilities and reinforce the case for their existing charter status.

- **Pattern 4:** parent-driven divestment (PDD) is the retraction of charter from a subsidiary by the parent company. To lower cost and centralise operations, parent companies may withdraw charters from some subsidiaries, which could lead to subsidiary capability decline. There are two ways to withdraw charters: one is to sell or close subsidiaries, which results in subsidiary capability loss; the other is to take away charters, while subsidiaries still exist. In this case, the associated capability developed for the withdrawn charter is lost, but the subsidiary can develop new capabilities for new charters. This is also known as charter renewal.

- **Pattern 5:** atrophy through subsidiary neglect (ASN) is the pattern in which a subsidiary loses charters because of the decline of its capabilities. This pattern results from two causes: (1) decline in absolute subsidiary capabilities, due to lack of sufficient attention to, or sense of, competition; (2) decline in relative subsidiary capabilities, because other subsidiaries have significantly improved their capabilities. As a result, the parent company transfers the charter to other, more competitive subsidiaries.

Birkinshaw noted that as a semi-autonomous entity, the subsidiary is not in complete control of its growth and development process. Three factors influence the evolution of subsidiaries: control of parent company, host environment and subsidiary choice (Figure 3.17). The first two drive passive adjustments, while the third is the initiative cause of development.

The control factors by the parent company include global strategy adjustment of the parent company, MNC global business reorganisation, subsidiary charter changes made by the parent company, and choices of centralisation or decentralisation by the parent company.

**Figure 3.17** Factors affecting overseas subsidiary evolution

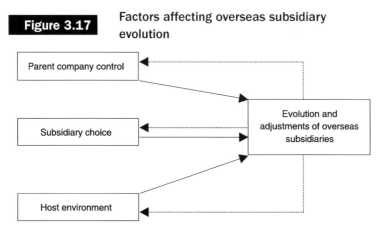

Source: Birkinshaw and Hood (1998b).

The choice factors of subsidiaries include subsidiary autonomy wishes, subsidiary entrepreneurial spirit and creative initiative, and subsidiary wishes to increase its significance in the MNC network.

The host environment factors include host culture environment, host country laws and regulations, host government intervention or support, market competition in the host country, and host country consumer demands.

In summary, subsidiary development scholars believe that the development of overseas subsidiaries is a dynamic process. Subsidiaries do not develop entirely in line with the parent company's strategic intent. Nor do they play a specific role for the long term in a host country. In time, MNC overseas subsidiaries might accumulate valuable resources and develop capabilities that will significantly enhance their status in their relationship with the parent company, and they could become as important as the parent companies. Meanwhile the role played by foreign subsidiaries can also change (Birkinshaw and Hood, 1997). Most MNC subsidiaries in China have contributed positively to the success of MNCs; however, in some cases, strategic blunders have resulted in a failure in China. For instance, MNCs such as Mosuoni, Whirlpool, Peugeot Automobile and Xerox have been forced to withdraw from China because of the strategic blunders of their subsidiaries.

# Notes

1 Ghoshal and Nohria (1993); Bartlett and Ghoshal (1989).
2 Porter, M.E. (2002) *National Competitive Advantage*. Translator: Mingxuan Li, etc. BeiJing: Huaxia Publishing House.
3 United Nations MNC Center (1994). *World Investment Report for 1993*. Translator: Xiangyin Chu, etc. Beijing: Foreign Trade Publication.
4 Changsi Shijing (1988). *Japanese enterprise overseas strategy*. Translator: Qinghua Lin, etc. Guangzhou: Huacheng Publishing House.
5 Ming Shangye (1992). *Sans Frontieres Time's Entrepreneurial Strategies*. Translator: Tiechui Li. Beijing: China Economic Publishing House.
6 Kottler, P., Fahey, L. and Jatusripitak, S. (1985). *The New Competition*. Englewood: Prentice-Hall.
7 Bartlett, C.A. and Ghoshal, S. (2002). *Cross-border management*. (2nd edition). Translator: Yeqing Ma, etc. Beijing: Demos Post and Telecommunications Publishing House.
8 Bartlett and Ghoshal (1986).
9 Birkinshaw and Hood (1998b).

# 4

# Empirical research on growth and development strategy

**Abstract:** In this chapter, we discuss our empirical research on growth and development strategy with premises and hypotheses. We explain the study methodology, including sample selection, operational definition and measurement for variables and statistical methods.

**Key words:** Empirical research, growth and development strategy, sample selection, measurement, statistical method.

To guide practice, research and public policy, the study of the growth and development strategy of MNC subsidiaries ought to be based on both robust theoretical foundation as well as first-hand empirical research. MNCs face a challenge of how to align their subsidiaries' functional and business strategies with the parent company's overall global strategy, while being flexible in satisfying the unique local characteristics and demands. In this chapter, the empirical aspects of the growth and development strategy of the MNC subsidiaries in China are investigated.

The growth and development strategy of MNC subsidiaries in China has its specific strategic scope and characteristics pertaining to issues such as:

- What are the motives for further investment in subsidiaries?

- Which factors influence subsidiary growth and development and to what extent?

**Figure 4.1**     Flowchart of the empirical analysis

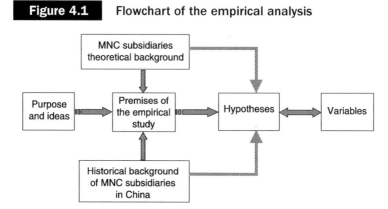

- What are the present competitive positions of subsidiaries in China?

- What are their competitive advantages?

- What are their prospects?

- What strategies do MNC subsidiaries in China choose to consolidate and enhance their competitiveness in China?

These issues will guide subsidiaries and MNCs to participate in competition in China. Figure 4.1 gives an overview of the research model guiding our empirical analysis.

## Analytical model

The empirical study is based on an analytical framework (Figure 4.2), identified and based on the theoretical as well as the historical backgrounds of MNC subsidiaries in China. The analytical framework is based on four premises and 15 conceptual components deriving from the MNC subsidiary S-SWOT analysis.

# Figure 4.2 Conceptual analytical framework

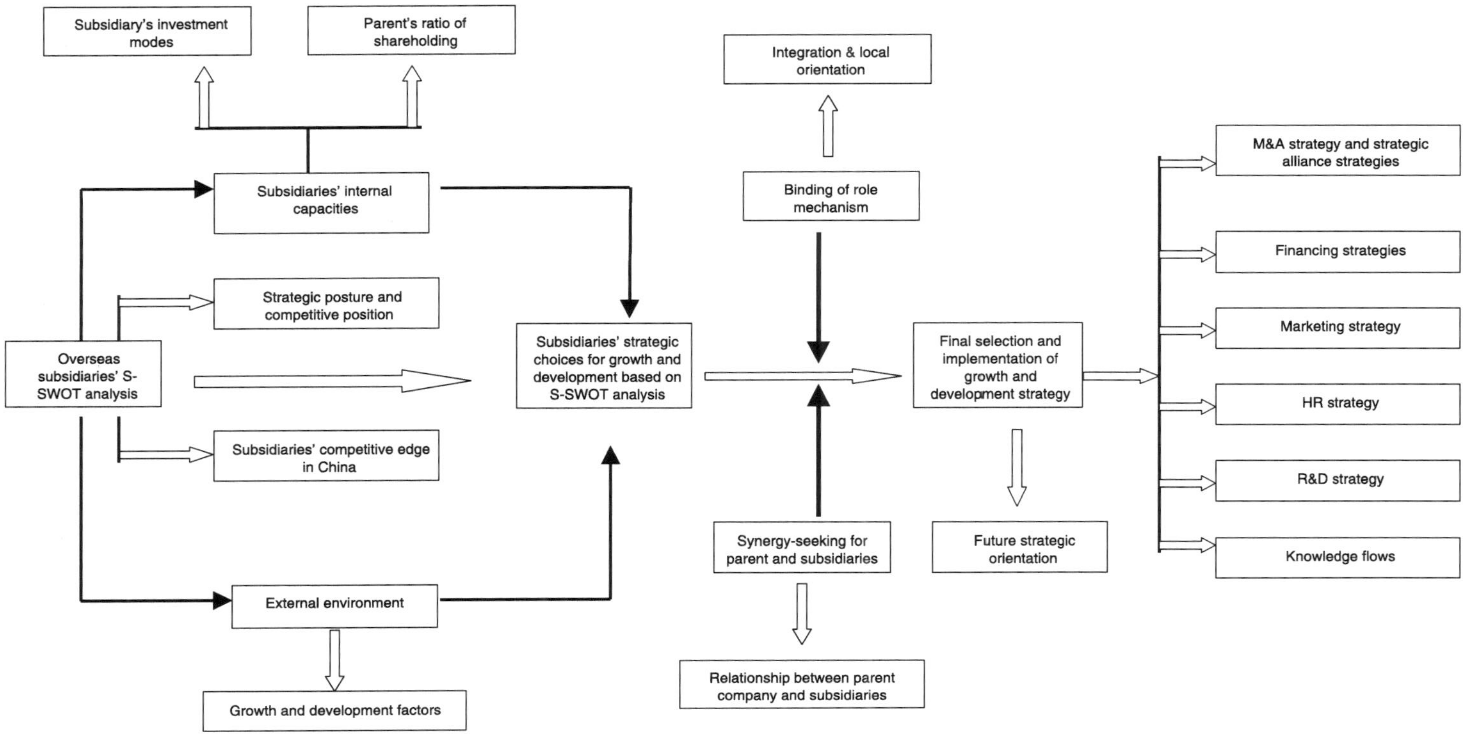

The four premises are:

1. MNC subsidiaries in China are controlled by the MNC, as a foreign parent company.
2. Growth and development strategies of the subsidiaries are a function of their analysis and understanding of SWOT from the perspective of their internal and external business environments.
3. Growth and development strategies manifest as corporate and functional strategies of the MNC subsidiaries.
4. There are country, industry and temporal effects in these strategies.

The 15 conceptual components are: (1) investment entry modes; (2) shareholding ratio; (3) growth and development strategy factors; (4) strategic posture or SWOT factors; (5) the most significant competitive advantages; (6) the most significant competitive advantage initiatives; (7) relationship with the parent company and with other subsidiaries; (8) integration and localisation; (9) mergers and acquisitions (M&As) and strategic alliances; (10) financing strategy; (11) knowledge transfer strategy; (12) marketing strategy; (13) human resource strategy; (14) R&D strategy; and (15) strategic blunders.

## Sample selection

A sample of 400 MNC subsidiaries was identified and approached using postal mail between October 2004 and April 2005, across more than 15 cities in China, including Shanghai, Beijing, Tianjin, Dalian, Fuzhou, Guangzhou, Hefei, Jinan, Changchun, Suzhou, Qingdao, Lianyungang, Anhui, Weihai and Songwan. Follow-up was conducted by telephone and email. To obtain greater participation from the MNC subsidiaries, support was elicited from the Ministry of Foreign Trade, provincial foreign economic bureaus and local municipality economic departments and offices in charge of the economic and technological zones. Support was also elicited from Seoul University and the South Korea Manufacturing Research Association to translate the instruments into Korean and to reach out to Korean MNC subsidiaries in China. By the end of May 2005, a total of 150 survey responses were obtained (37.5 per cent), of which 128 were usable (32 per cent). In addition to the surveys, interviews were conducted with many of the subsidiaries.

Table 4.1 gives the demographic of the respondents. Of the 128 respondents, 26 were board-level (board chairman, vice chairman, member or CEO), and 62 belonged to the top management teams. Twenty-eight of the MNC subsidiaries represented by these respondents were from the USA; 22 from Japan; 25 from the European Union; 43 from South Korea; and 10 from other nations. The wholly and majority foreign-owned MNC subsidiaries account for 97.7 per cent among all the sampled MNC subsidiaries.

# Statistical methods

Several statistical methods were used for data analysis using SPSS software: factor analysis, cluster analysis, correlation coefficient analysis, independent samples t-test method and independent non-parametric test, ANOVA analysis and the weighted average method.

# Hypotheses on the behaviours of MNC subsidiaries in China

To guide our empirical investigation, we formulate a set of hypotheses on the behaviour of MNC subsidiaries in China,

**Table 4.1** Sample characteristics

| Firm characteristics | Firm category | Firm numbers | Percentage (%) |
|---|---|---|---|
| Country origin | South Korea | 43 | 33.6 |
| | USA | 28 | 21.9 |
| | European Union | 25 | 19.5 |
| | Japan | 22 | 17.2 |
| | Others | 10 | 7.8 |
| Degree of foreign ownership | Foreign whole | 91 | 71.1 |
| | Foreign majority | 34 | 26.6 |
| | Foreign minority | 3 | 2.3 |
| Headquarters location | China headquarters | 33 | 25.8 |
| | Global headquarters | 31 | 24.2 |
| | Asia Pacific headquarters | 27 | 21.1 |
| | Big China headquarters | 7 | 5.5 |
| | Missing data | 17 | 13.3 |
| | Others | 13 | 10.2 |
| Industry | Electronics | 35 | 27.3 |
| | Textile | 23 | 18.0 |
| | Chemistry and pharmaceutical | 15 | 11.7 |
| | Iron, steel, mechanics and engineering | 13 | 10.2 |
| | Auto manufacturing | 9 | 7.0 |
| | Food and beverages | 9 | 7.0 |
| | Commerce and trade | 7 | 5.5 |
| | Transportation | 5 | 3.9 |
| | Telecommunications | 3 | 2.3 |
| | Finance and insurance | 2 | 1.6 |
| | Consulting | 2 | 1.6 |
| | Others | 2 | 1.6 |
| | Gasoline and mining | 1 | 0.8 |
| | Real estate | 1 | 0.8 |
| | Mass communication | 1 | 0.8 |
| Subject ranks | Board chairman | 3 | 2.3 |
| | Board vice chairman | 4 | 3.1 |
| | Board member | 6 | 4.7 |
| | CEO | 13 | 10.2 |
| | Vice CEO | 16 | 12.5 |
| | Department manager | 46 | 35.9 |
| | Others | 31 | 24.2 |
| | Missing data | 9 | 7.0 |
| Firm age | Less than 5 years | 43 | 33.6 |
| | 5–9 years | 49 | 38.3 |
| | 10–15 years | 22 | 17.2 |
| | More than 15 years | 10 | 7.8 |
| | Missing data | 4 | 3.1 |

corresponding to each of the 15 conceptual components in the analytical framework. Operational measures for each of the hypotheses are also specified. The following chapters discuss these hypotheses and results in two parts: (1) strategic intent focusing on investment and competitive factors; (2) corporate and functional strategies.

# Part 3
# Hypothesis testing and analysis

# 5

# Strategic intent: investment and competitive factors

**Abstract:** In this chapter, we investigate investment and competitive factors for strategic intent, including investment mode, shareholding ratio, growth and development factors, competitive mandate, competitive advantages and competitive advantage initiatives. We present findings and analysis on strategic intent, and summarise them in a table.

**Key words:** Investment and competitive factors, strategic intent, investment mode, shareholding ratio, growth and development factors, competitive mandate, competitive advantages, hypotheses, findings, competitive advantage.

## Hypotheses

### Hypothesis 1: investment mode

- 1.1: The entry investment mode varies significantly across MNC subsidiaries in China, depending *on the national origin of their parent company.*

- 1.2: The entry investment mode varies significantly across MNC subsidiaries in China, depending *on the time of their entry in China.*

- 1.3: The present investment mode of MNC subsidiaries in China is significantly related to their industry market share.

Three investment modes were studied: (1) wholly owned (95 per cent or more foreign equity shareholding); (2) joint ventures (50–94 per cent foreign ownership); and (3) minority controlling ownership in joint ventures (less than 50 per cent foreign ownership). Coding was done for the investment mode at the time of first entry of the MNC subsidiary in China and at the time of the study.

## Hypothesis 2: shareholding ratio

Respondents were asked about the direction of change in the foreign share of equity since entry, and the factors in the changes in foreign shareholding ratio. No hypothesis was advanced.

Factors in the changes in the shareholding ratio were measured using a five-point scale (1 = strongly disagree; 5 = strongly agree).

## Hypothesis 3: growth and development factors

Respondents were asked about the important growth and development factors, key growth indicators and significance of various investment motives for MNC subsidiaries in China. No specific hypothesis was advanced.

Growth and development factors were measured using the items in Table 5.1 on a five-point scale (1 = very insignificant; 5 = very significant).

Growth indicators were measured using the items in Table 5.2 on a five-point scale (1 = very insignificant; 5 = very significant).

Investment expansion motives were measured using the items in Table 5.3 on a five-point scale (1 = very insignificant; 5 = very significant).

**Table 5.1** Growth and development factors

| Internal factors | | | |
|---|---|---|---|
| Internal management issues | Attraction to senior international talents | Relationship with the local government | Relationship with the local public |
| External factors | | | |
| Local government factors | Legal, social and cultural factors | Market factors | Parent factor |
| Host country's tax policy | Cultural differences | Quality of local staff | Strategic requirements of the parent company |
| Local protectionism | Protection of intellectual property rights | Competition situation in the local market | |
| | | Financing constraints | |
| | | Raw material supply constraints | |

**Table 5.2** Growth indicators for MNC subsidiaries in China

| |
|---|
| Sales volume |
| Investment scale |
| Market shares |
| Profit |
| Return on investment |
| R&D investment |

**Table 5.3** Investment expansion motives for MNC subsidiaries in China

| |
|---|
| Seek greater profits |
| Expand production base in China |
| Get more market shares in China |
| Maintain cost advantages |
| Compete with other MNCs |
| Increase the R&D ability in China |
| Follow existing clients |

## *Hypothesis 4: competitive mandate*

Respondents were asked about the perception of other MNC subsidiaries in China versus the local Chinese enterprises as competitors, the areas along the value chain the subsidiary is engaged in, significance of alternative performance measures and the significance of various factors in the strategic position the subsidiary held in the MNC network. No specific hypothesis was advanced.

Performance measures expected by the parent company from MNC subsidiaries in China were measured on a five-point scale (1 = very insignificant; 5 = very significant) using items in Table 5.4.

**Table 5.4**     Items used for performance measures

| |
|---|
| Revenue |
| Profit |
| Market shares |
| Product quality indicators |
| Return on investment |
| Customer satisfaction |
| Safety of employees |
| Completion of planned budget |
| Shareholders' rate of return |
| Relations with local government and the public |
| Staff training |
| Productivity indicators |
| Service target |
| Social responsibility |
| Worker turnover |
| Relation with parent company |
| Company R&D |

## *Hypothesis 5: competitive advantages*

- 5.1: Competitive advantages of MNC subsidiaries in China differ depending *on the national origin of their parent company.*
- 5.2: Competitive advantages of MNC subsidiaries in China differ depending *on their industry of operation.*
- 5.3: Competitive advantages of MNC subsidiaries in China differ depending *on their relative market share.*[1]
- 5.4: Competitive advantages of MNC subsidiaries in China differ depending *on their perceived SWOT.*

The competitive advantages were identified using responses on a five-point scale (1 = very insignificant; 5 = very significant), showing the perceived advantage of the MNC subsidiary over its competitors on the items in Table 5.5.

**Table 5.5**   Items used for competitive advantage

| |
|---|
| Quality control |
| Firm image |
| Quality of management team |
| Competitive advantages within MNC network |
| Function and price ratio for products |
| Service |
| Core technology |
| Brand |
| Firm information capacity |
| Customer relationship management |
| Customer demand satisfaction |
| Products portfolio |
| Cost control |
| R&D capabilities |
| Relationship with local government |
| Raw materials/parts procurement |
| Capital operation capabilities |
| Logistics |
| Control of distribution channels |

## Hypothesis 6: competitive advantage initiatives

- 6.1: Competitive advantage initiatives of MNC subsidiaries in China differ depending *on the national origin of their parent company.*
- 6.2: Competitive advantage initiatives of MNC subsidiaries in China differ depending *on their industry of operation.*
- 6.3: Competitive advantage initiatives of MNC subsidiaries in China differ depending *on their relative market share.*
- 6.4: Competitive advantage initiatives of MNC subsidiaries in China differ depending *on their perceived SWOT.*

The competitive advantage initiatives were identified using responses on a five-point scale (1 = very insignificant; 5 = very significant), showing the initiatives focused on by the MNC subsidiary.

# Findings and analysis

## Hypothesis 1: investment entry mode

### Context

The choice of entry mode is an important decision of the global expansion of MNCs. The decision involves not only entry barriers and cost, but also overall business and development strategy of an MNC. MNCs of different country origins may therefore choose different entry modes. Further, the MNC capabilities and the host business environment and legal policy can change over time. Accordingly, MNCs' entry modes may differ at different time periods even within the same region.

In the early 1980s, China began presenting huge potential for many MNCs in the world. China started to implement reforms and an open-door policy that shaped its market

**Figure 5.1**   MNC entry investment modes, n = 118

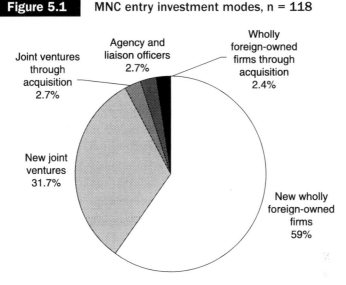

economy. After an exploratory phase of investment, MNCs began large-scale direct investments in China. The MNC entry modes of the 123 sampled subsidiaries were divided into five major categories: new joint ventures (39), new wholly foreign-owned firms (73), wholly foreign-owned firms through acquisition (3), joint ventures through acquisition (4), and agency and liaison offices (4).

Newly established subsidiaries, foreign-owned and joint ventures account for 98 per cent of the sample. The number of new subsidiaries is significantly greater than that of subsidiaries through mergers or acquisitions for two major reasons: China's industry policy restrictions and a lack of suitable targets for acquisition or merger. As a result, acquiring existing firms is not the first choice for most MNCs seeking to establish their subsidiaries in China.

## Test of hypotheses

**Hypothesis 1.1: the first investment entry method varies significantly across MNC subsidiaries in China, depending on the time of their entry.**

**Table 5.6** First entry method by time of entry, chi square test

| Statistics | Value | df | p-value |
|---|---|---|---|
| Likelihood ratio chi square | 11.856 | 4 | 0.018 |
| N | 119 | | |

The first investment entry method and years of operation are correlated, $\chi^2$ (4, $\underline{N}$ = 119) = 29.922, $\underline{p}$ = 0<0.05 (see Table 5.6).

**Hypothesis 1.2: the first investment entry method varies significantly across MNC subsidiaries in China, depending on the national origin of their parent company.**

The first investment entry method and national origin of the parent company are correlated, $\chi^2$ (3, N = 114) = 10.594, p < 0.05. Table 5.7 presents cross-tabs of entry modes across different countries of origin.

The entry forms for MNCs from Japan and South Korea were significantly different from those for MNCs from the US and the European Union. The former showed a significantly stronger preference for new wholly foreign-owned firms, relative to new joint ventures. MNCs from Europe and the United States experienced greater cultural differences, which resulted in their greater willingness to use

**Table 5.7** First entry method by country

| | US | Japan | EU | Korea |
|---|---|---|---|---|
| New wholly foreign-owned firms | 12 | 13 | 11 | 33 |
| New joint ventures | 11 | 7 | 11 | 7 |
| Wholly foreign-owned firms through acquisition | 0 | 1 | 1 | 1 |
| Joint venture through acquisition or merger | 2 | 0 | 1 | 0 |

| Table 5.8 | Average tenure by country |

| Country of origin | Average tenure |
| --- | --- |
| US | 9.00 |
| Japan | 8.10 |
| EU | 15.00 |
| Korea | 6.88 |
| Overall | 9.12 |

joint ventures when first entering China. Chinese partners offered help in lowering entry barriers and effectively understanding Chinese culture. On the other hand, Japan and South Korea share cultural commonalities with China. MNCs from these two nations had a lower need for local partners' help with cultural issues. Thus, they showed a marked preference for the new wholly foreign-owned firms.

Table 5.8 presents average tenure of MNC subsidiaries across different country origins.

MNCs from the US and the European Union entered China, on average, earlier than MNCs from Japan and South Korea. Since China has gradually opened its markets to the outside world, MNCs entering later enjoyed a more favourable regulatory environment and fewer policy constraints. This also contributed to the choice of wholly foreign-owned subsidiaries by Japan and South Korea. MNCs from Europe and the United States entered China earlier and experienced a less supportive policy environment that required greater use of joint ventures.

**Hypothesis 1.3: the present investment mode of MNC subsidiaries in China is significantly related to their industry market share.**

The present investment mode and the relative market share of MNC subsidiaries in China are not related, $\chi^2$ (28, N = 128) = 29.922, p > 0.10 (Table 5.9).

| Table 5.9 | Present investment mode by relative market share, chi square test |
|---|---|

| Statistics | Value | df | p-value |
|---|---|---|---|
| Likelihood ratio chi square | 29.922 | 28 | 0.367 |
| N | 128 | | |

## Hypothesis 2: shareholding ratio

### Context

The shareholding ratio of MNC subsidiaries in China is an important decision involving risk-sharing, allocation of resources, knowledge commitment and organisational control. Respondents were asked about the direction of the foreign equity change. We found that more MNC subsidiaries in China have increased share of foreign equity since their entry, as opposed to decreasing. MNCs want to have better control over their subsidiaries in China. Of n = 64, 42 (65.6 per cent) did not change foreign shareholding ratio. Four reduced their ratio and another four became wholly foreign-owned. A total of 18 (28.2 per cent) increased their ratio (see Table 5.10).

No change in the ownership structure of the 65.6 per cent of the subsidiaries is due to one of two major reasons: (1) the parent company has no plan to invest more or divest because

| Table 5.10 | Changes in foreign shareholding ratio statistics |
|---|---|

| | N | % of valid N |
|---|---|---|
| Reduction in foreign equity ownership | 4 | 6.3 |
| No change | 42 | 65.6 |
| Increase in foreign equity ownership | 14 | 21.9 |
| Change to foreign wholly owned subsidiaries | 4 | 6.3 |
| Total | 64 | 100.0 |

the joint venture is in the probation period or in the norming stage; or (2) although MNCs have the intention to invest more to get better control, China's policy and related legal restrictions in many sectors prohibit MNCs from having more than 50 per cent of the shares in their joint ventures. In the latter case, MNCs usually use subtle ways to achieve effective control.

Consider the case of the vehicle industry, where we investigated three enterprises: Jinan China Hugh Ltd, Changchun Bombardier Railway Vehicle Co. Ltd and FAW-Volkswagen Automotive Co. In the vehicle industry, the legal policy restricted foreign ownership to no more than 50 per cent. However, MNCs in the investigated enterprises achieved substantial control by way of their branding and technology. We can predict that when the policy restrictions are removed, foreign investment will increase considerably towards greater or even total equity control. Therefore, these subsidiaries will join the MNC global system for more tax savings and global strategic services for MNCs.

Reduction of shareholding by MNCs in 6.3 per cent is due to one of two major reasons: (1) the joint venture not operating properly and not meeting the performance requirements of the MNC; or (2) the joint venture having very good operating performance with promising industry prospects. The MNC wants to increase equity to strengthen control or increase profits from the joint venture, but is restricted by some policy or regulation reason. Therefore, the MNCs decide to reduce their investment to withdraw funds and set up a new wholly owned subsidiary to achieve their strategic intent.

## Reasons for change in shareholding ratio

The parent company's global strategy is the most significant factor in changes in the shareholding ratio of MNC subsidiaries in China: 62.5 per cent of executives believed

MNCs need to adjust their global strategy, and thus control over subsidiaries' management and operations, in accordance with the global environmental changes. From Table 5.11, two related factors – adjustment of the parent company's global strategy and change of subsidiary importance in the parent network system – have means greater than 3.50, and at least 50 per cent of the respondents identify them as significant or very significant (see Table 5.11).

We investigated the motives for changing shareholding ratio for two categories of MNC subsidiaries: those where ratio was increased and those where it was decreased (Table 5.12). For the MNC subsidiaries that experienced increase in their shareholding ratio, the key factors were parent company's global strategy adjustment and change in the

| **Table 5.11** | Reasons for change in foreign shareholding ratio |

| The reasons for changes in the shareholding ratio | N | Mean | SD | % reporting 4 or 5, on a 5-point scale |
|---|---|---|---|---|
| Global strategy adjustment of the parent company | 24 | 3.71 | 1.083 | 62.5 |
| Change of control for core technology and resources | 20 | 3.55 | 0.887 | 40.0 |
| Change of subsidiary importance in the parent network system | 20 | 3.50 | 1.192 | 50.0 |
| Difference in strategic goal for joint ventures | 18 | 3.39 | 1.145 | 44.4 |
| Changes of company performance | 26 | 3.35 | 1.294 | 42.3 |
| Change of host country regulatory environment | 21 | 3.24 | 0.995 | 38.1 |
| Change of host country market environment | 20 | 3.10 | 1.021 | 30.0 |
| Cultural conflict in business management | 19 | 2.95 | 0.780 | 26.3 |

Note: 1 = strongly disagree; 5 = strongly agree.

| Table 5.12 | Reasons for change in foreign shareholding ratio by direction of change | | |

| Reasons for ownership changes | Shareholding ratio increase group Mean (n) | Shareholding ratio decrease group Mean (n) |
|---|---|---|
| MNC global strategy adjustment | 3.91 (11) | 3.33 (3) |
| Change of subsidiary performance | 3.75 (12) | 3.00 (3) |
| Strategic goal difference of joint venture partners | 3.67 (9) | 3.33 (3) |
| Change of significance in MNC network | 3.60 (10) | 3.33 (3) |
| Change of control over core technology and resources | 3.60 (10) | 3.67 (3) |
| Change of host country market environment | 3.00 (10) | 3.33 (3) |
| Change of host regulatory environment | 3.00 (11) | 3.67 (3) |
| Cross-cultural conflict in subsidiary management | 3.00 (9) | 2.67 (3) |

performance of the subsidiaries. For the MNC subsidiaries that experienced decrease in their shareholding ratio, the key factors were change in the regulatory environment in China and in the control over core technology and resources.

## Hypothesis 3: growth and development factors

### Context

We found that the respondents identified the parent company's strategic requirements as the most significant growth and development factor; more than 70 per cent of the respondents identified this as significant. Subsidiaries serve as an implementation vehicle for an MNC seeking to achieve its global strategic goals. Thus any adjustment in

MNC strategy change affects the growth and development strategy of these subsidiaries.

Meanwhile, to fit in with the cultural and social demands of the Chinese local markets, the subsidiaries must cultivate and nurture relations with the local government and the public. Relations with local government and the public, quality of local staff and host country tax policy are also all rated more than 3.50 and reported to be significant by at least 50 per cent of the respondents. Interestingly, financing constraints are identified as the least significant factor, with a mean of less than 3.0, and deemed a significant factor by less than a third of the respondents (see Table 5.13). However, most executives hold factors such as cultural differences,

**Table 5.13**    Growth and development factors statistics

| | N | Mean | SD | % reporting 4 or 5, on a 5-point scale |
|---|---|---|---|---|
| Parent company strategic requirements | 96 | 3.93 | 0.909 | 70.9 |
| Relations with local government and public | 91 | 3.82 | 0.973 | 62.7 |
| Quality of local staff | 94 | 3.71 | 0.785 | 57.4 |
| Host country tax policy | 93 | 3.65 | 1.007 | 54.9 |
| Firm internal issues | 96 | 3.50 | 1.016 | 47.9 |
| Intellectual property rights protection | 90 | 3.47 | 1.210 | 50.0 |
| Attraction to international senior talents | 92 | 3.34 | 1.051 | 42.4 |
| Local market competition | 99 | 3.31 | 1.027 | 44.4 |
| Constraints on raw material supply | 98 | 3.30 | 1.177 | 44.9 |
| Local protectionism | 94 | 3.05 | 0.999 | 31.9 |
| Cultural differences | 98 | 3.02 | 1.084 | 34.7 |
| Financing constraints | 92 | 2.97 | 1.253 | 32.6 |

Note: 1 = very insignificant; 5 = very significant.

financing constraints and local protectionism as not significant for their operations in China. The average age of sampled MNC subsidiaries is 8.22 years and many of them have gone beyond the emerging and survival period. They have accumulated rich experiences in dealing with cultural conflict issues and financing difficulties and thus these issues are no longer considered important obstacles for their operations.

## Test of hypotheses

**Hypothesis 3.1: the growth and development factors of MNC subsidiaries in China differ depending on the national origin of their parent company.**

When MNC subsidiaries design and implement their growth and development strategy, they are influenced by the cultural and other characteristics of the parent company. Subsidiaries of the MNCs from different national origins have different perceptions of the significant factors in strategy formulation process. We also ran a frequency analysis and compared the mean scores from the respondents from four different national origins (Table 5.14). T-test of difference showed several significant differences. Specifically:

1. US subsidiaries are significantly more influenced by firm internal management factors than subsidiaries from the EU, Japan or Korea.

2. US and EU subsidiaries are significantly more influenced by competition in local market, intellectual property protection and attraction of international senior talent factors than the subsidiaries from Japan or Korea.

3. Japanese subsidiaries are least influenced by the quality of local staff.

Further, the means on all factors are generally higher for US subsidiaries. US MNCs have paid special attention to various

| Table 5.14 | Growth and development factors by country |

| Influential factors | US | Japan | EU | Korea |
|---|---|---|---|---|
| 1 Competition in local market | 3.72 | 3.13 | 3.24 | 3.09 |
| 2 Local protectionism | 3.36 | 2.93 | 3.29 | 2.73 |
| 3 Firm internal management | 3.78 | 3.57 | 3.11 | 3.48 |
| 4 Quality of local staff | 3.86 | 3.40 | 3.63 | 3.87 |
| 5 Attraction of international senior talents | 3.59 | 2.88 | 3.63 | 3.26 |
| 6 Intellectual property protection | 4.00 | 3.07 | 3.61 | 3.19 |

strategic factors affecting their subsidiaries in China because of the length of investment and strategic uniqueness. The average age of the sampled US subsidiaries is 9.00 years, which is higher than those from Japan (8.1 years) and South Korea (6.88 years). US subsidiaries have integrated to a larger degree into the Chinese system and markets. In addition, many US MNCs entering China have used a complementary investment approach, in which spare parts, facilities and management practices have been localised. This has allowed US subsidiaries to be very flexible in responding to both internal and external environmental challenges. They have thus become more sensitive to environment changes than subsidiaries from other countries.

Conversely, the means on all factors are generally lower for subsidiaries from Japan and South Korea. These subsidiaries have had a shorter time operating in China, yet experience less vulnerability to external environmental changes because of the cultural and geographical proximity. Japan and South Korea have a long history of cultural interactions with China because they are neighbours and their subsidiaries in China can adapt to the changes more quickly than subsidiaries whose parent company is located in Western countries.

## Motives for additional MNC investments

MNCs carried out their second and subsequent rounds of investment for their subsidiaries in China after completion of the initial investment. The motives for additional direct investment reflect MNC strategic intentions in China. Table 5.15 shows that profit-seeking is the most significant motive for further investments by MNC subsidiaries in China, with a mean of more than 4.0, and nearly 75 per cent of the respondents identifying as significant. Other significant factors include expansion of production base in China and securing more market share in China. Maintaining cost advantage and competing with other MNCs are also significant factors. On the other hand, enhancing R&D capability in China and following existing clients in China are not that significant (see Table 5.15).

We conducted a factor analysis of the microeconomic motives, using the orthogonal Varimax rotation of principal component method (Table 5.16). Two factors emerged:

**Table 5.15**   Further investment motives

| Investment expansion motives | N | Mean | Standard deviation | % reporting 4 or 5 on a 5-point scale |
|---|---|---|---|---|
| Seek greater profits | 95 | 4.03 | 1.005 | 74.7 |
| Expand production base in China | 94 | 3.87 | 1.008 | 66.0 |
| Get more market share in China | 91 | 3.87 | 0.991 | 68.1 |
| Maintain cost advantages | 89 | 3.78 | 1.085 | 61.8 |
| Compete with other MNCs | 78 | 3.44 | 1.180 | 52.6 |
| Increase the R&D ability in China | 80 | 3.36 | 1.058 | 38.8 |
| Follow existing clients | 81 | 3.31 | 1.261 | 46.9 |

Note: 1 = strongly disagree; 5 = strongly agree.

scale-oriented investment factor (seeking profits, production base expansion, market share expansion, low cost advantages) and competition-oriented investment factor (global competitors, R&D capability enhancement and following existing clients). These two factors explain 64.07 per cent of the total variance with the first explaining 47.08 per cent and the second 16.99 per cent.

The average scores for the scale-oriented factor exceed those for the competition-oriented factor. Thus, the overriding driving force for MNCs to make extra direct investments in China is to use low cost advantages for their rapid expansion and lay a solid foundation for future development. Because of its low cost of raw materials, labour, land and other factors of production, MNCs make China their global manufacturing base. They take advantage of China's low cost for rapid expansion and to reduce global production costs. MNCs enjoy better product quality and brand image, which helps snatch market share from the domestic enterprises. Earning profits is a necessary condition to support sustained development in these situations. If the payback period is too long, the cost of opportunities for further development is huge. Therefore, MNCs invest additional funds in those

| Table 5.16 | Factor analysis of the further investment motives | |
|---|---|---|

| Microeconomic motives | Main components | |
|---|---|---|
| | 1 | 2 |
| Seeking maximised profits | 0.775 | 0.127 |
| Expanding production bases in China | 0.762 | 0.325 |
| Expanding market share in China | 0.813 | 0.035 |
| Sustaining low cost advantages | 0.526 | 0.492 |
| Competing global competitors | 0.287 | 0.818 |
| Enhancing R&D capabilities in China | 0.427 | 0.490 |
| Following existing clients | − 0.037 | 0.909 |

activities (production and sales) that yield highest return rate, shifting from more strategic priorities in their early entry decision where they are willing to forego profits to a focus on return on investment in their later investment decisions.

Though scale-oriented factors are important, neglect of competition-oriented factors can cause MNC subsidiaries in China to lose their competitive advantages. The overall capacity of Chinese markets is very large, but some local markets have been divided among a few winners after a fierce competitive war. In such a situation, if MNCs want to expand sales or increase market share, they need to increase research and development efforts and accelerate new lines of products while reducing the cost of production for old products. They need to get ready for more brutal competition for survival. Therefore, in future, we expect that the focus of MNC investments will shift to competition-oriented factors such as R&D and customer relationship management.

## Hypothesis 4: competitive mandate

### Perceived competitors

We found that MNC subsidiaries in China perceive other MNC subsidiaries in China to be stronger competitors than are the local Chinese enterprises. To the question 'who are the biggest competitors?' 69 of the 97 valid respondents identified other MNC subsidiaries in China and only 28 identified local Chinese enterprises.

### Value chain activities

MNC subsidiaries in China are engaged in activities along the primary value chain: manufacturing (20.8 per cent), sales (14.5 per cent), service (7.8 per cent), R&D (13.3 per cent) and procurement (12.9 per cent), as opposed to

**Table 5.17**   Types of value chain activity

| Type of value chain activity | N | % |
|---|---|---|
| Manufacturing centre | 53 | 20.8% |
| Sales centre | 37 | 14.5% |
| R&D centre | 34 | 13.3% |
| Procurement centre | 33 | 12.9% |
| Market centre | 24 | 9.4% |
| Training centre | 21 | 8.2% |
| Service centre | 20 | 7.8% |
| Investment management centre | 16 | 6.3% |
| Finance centre | 16 | 6.3% |

supporting value chain – finance (6.3 per cent), investment management (6.3 per cent) or training (8.2 per cent) (see Table 5.17).

## Performance criteria

We also investigated what performance indicators the parent company cares most about for MNC subsidiaries in China, using a five-point scale (1 = not concerned; 5 = very concerned). Revenue and profit are the most important performance measures from the perspective of MNC parents, with a mean of more than 4.0, and at least 80 per cent of the respondents reporting them as significant. Market share, product quality, return on investment and customer satisfaction are other important measures.

Conversely, human resources, R&D, relation with parent company and social responsibility are of limited importance. The parent companies have shown less concern to the R&D of their subsidiaries, as that requires huge funding and does not yield any short-term results. Also, R&D indicators are not easily measured and evaluated. Moreover, China was relatively weak in scientific research at the time when most

MNCs started to invest and did not have the necessary conditions to become a regional research and development centre for the MNCs. Thus, R&D was housed by most MNCs outside of China. This greatly hindered the technological progress for local development and hurt the subsidiaries' long-term growth. Now many MNCs are putting priorities on local R&D with increasing investment.

MNC subsidiaries in China can only maximise their interests after meeting the strategic requirements of the parent company for its global manoeuvre. Initially, when MNCs entered China's market, the priority for the subsidiaries was market expansion and brand products promotion, as opposed

**Table 5.18**    Performance criteria expected by MNC parents

| Performance measures | Mean | % reporting 4 or 5 on a 5-point scale |
| --- | --- | --- |
| Revenue | 4.26 | 80.47% |
| Profit | 4.25 | 85.16% |
| Market share | 4.23 | 74.22% |
| Product quality | 4.21 | 74.22% |
| Return on investment | 4.19 | 75.00% |
| Customer satisfaction | 4.09 | 74.22% |
| Safety of employees | 3.97 | 72.66% |
| Completion of planned budget | 4.09 | 83.59% |
| Shareholders' rate of return | 4.07 | 68.75% |
| Relations with local government and the public | 3.95 | 74.22% |
| Staff training | 3.94 | 76.56% |
| Productivity | 3.92 | 70.31% |
| Service target | 3.91 | 67.19% |
| Social responsibility | 3.88 | 71.09% |
| Worker turnover | 3.75 | 69.53% |
| Relation with parent company | 3.74 | 70.31% |
| Company R&D | 3.74 | 67.97% |

Note: 1 = not concerned at all; 5 = very concerned.

to sales revenues and profits. However, the parent company performance indicators for MNC subsidiaries in China have now shifted to sales, profits, return on investment, market share and product quality. This suggests that MNC subsidiaries in China have entered a new stage of development.

Further, sales revenues, investment scale and market share are the three most significant performance measures of MNC subsidiaries in China from the perspective of the subsidiaries, with means of more than 3.50, and with at least 50 per cent of the respondents identifying them as significant. In contrast, profitability, return on investment and R&D investment are less significant (see Table 5.19).

Sales, investment scale and market shares have driven the growth momentum for MNC subsidiaries in China. There are three reasons for a focus on these indicators: (1) MNC subsidiaries in China are either in the growth stage or just getting started. They need a lot of talent and a large amount of capital investment to establish corporate image, strengthen branding and expand sales channels. (2) China has huge market potential. MNC subsidiaries in China are engaging in expanding their production base and sales to acquire more

**Table 5.19** Performance measures focused on by MNC subsidiaries

|  | N | Mean | Standard deviation | % reporting 4 or 5 on a 5-point scale |
|---|---|---|---|---|
| Sales revenues | 109 | 3.77 | 0.878 | 63.3 |
| Investment scale | 96 | 3.67 | 0.842 | 60.4 |
| Market shares | 96 | 3.61 | 0.875 | 54.1 |
| Profit | 110 | 3.52 | 0.916 | 48.1 |
| Return on investment | 92 | 3.40 | 0.839 | 43.5 |
| R&D investment | 82 | 3.28 | 0.893 | 37.8 |

Note: 1 = very insignificant; 5 = very significant.

market share. Their strategic priority is not the pursuit of profit or rate of return on investments at this time. (3) The parent companies of MNCs assess the performance of subsidiaries using such indicators as sales volumes, investment scale and market share. These performance indicators are easy to measure, quantify and implement. These appraisal indicators affect the management decision choices and operation activities of subsidiaries in China. To survive, grow and meet parent company expectations, subsidiaries have invested tremendously in these areas, both in money and human capital.

The subsidiaries poor in sales volumes and market shares face serious consequences of less support from the parent company and risk being merged, acquired or even sold off. A typical withdrawal case is that of Whirlpool. Though Whirlpool acquired Snowflakes Appliances with investment of more than $30 million, when the sales and market performance expectations were not met, the latter was sold for only $2 million as Whirlpool withdrew from China. Another withdrawal case is that of Dutch dairy giant Friesland Kraft Parmalat. At the time of its entry into the Chinese market, this Dutch MNC projected to make profit from the sixth year, but its subsidiary suffered losses for nine consecutive years with stagnated sales and unsatisfactory market share. The Dutch MNC finally decided to divest and withdraw from the Chinese market at a huge loss – allowing the competitors to enjoy substantial gains in their own market share and leadership positions.

There are, however, substantial differences in the importance given by the MNC parent companies versus the subsidiaries to rate of return. While parent companies put a stronger priority on rate of return, the subsidiaries show a lower concern for profitability and their rate of return performance is not as good as expected by the parent companies.

## Competitive posture

Based on the perception of SWOT of the respondents, we conducted a cluster analysis to identify three types of strategic postures for MNC subsidiaries in China: strength–threat cluster, strength–opportunity cluster and weakness–opportunity cluster. SWOT analysis showed 24 sampled firms to be in the weakness–threat quadrant (21.8 per cent), 62 in the strength–opportunity quadrant (53.4 per cent) and 24 in the weakness–opportunity quadrant (21.8 per cent) (Figure 5.2).

A majority of the MNC subsidiaries remain in the original favourable strength–opportunity position. They share similar competitive advantages of fit between overall external environmental factors and internal organisational core competences. However, because of changes in external environmental factors and competition status over the years, many firms have shifted into weakness–opportunity and strength–threat positions (43.6 per cent total) from their original strength–opportunity status. This is the result of

**Figure 5.2** Classification of subsidiaries by perceived SWOT

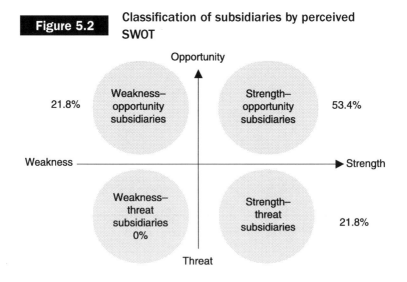

| Table 5.20 | Classification of subsidiaries by perceived SWOT | | | |

| Country origin | SWOT type | | | Total |
|---|---|---|---|---|
| | ST | SO | WO | |
| US | 6 | 16 | 2 | 24 |
| | 25.0% | 66.7% | 8.3% | 100.0% |
| Japan | 6 | 6 | 4 | 16 |
| | 37.5% | 37.5% | 25.0% | 100.0% |
| EU | 5 | 16 | 3 | 24 |
| | 20.8% | 66.7% | 12.5% | 100.0% |
| South Korea | 6 | 17 | 13 | 36 |
| | 16.7% | 47.2% | 36.1% | 100.0% |

interactions of internal capabilities and external situation changes, and the long-term fitness test.

Table 5.20 shows that a majority of the US and EU subsidiaries are in the strength–opportunity quadrant. They are more optimistic about their external environment and internal strengths. South Korean firms have a comparatively greater tendency to be in the weakness–opportunity quadrant, while the Japanese firms have a comparatively greater tendency to be in the strength–threat quadrant. South Korean firms are less confident about their internal capability to capitalise on the external opportunities, while the Japanese firms are concerned about the threats in the Chinese market that might inhibit optimal exploitation of their internal capability.

## Strategic position in MNC network

Firm-specific factors are more important than the parent company and host environment factors in the strategic

| Table 5.21 | Factors influencing strategic position of subsidiaries in MNC network |

| Competitive advantage factors | Mean |
|---|---|
| Quality control | 3.97 |
| Firm image | 3.90 |
| Quality of management team | 3.84 |
| Competitive advantages within MNC network | 3.82 |
| Function and price ratio for products | 3.77 |
| Service | 3.81 |
| Core technology | 3.81 |
| Brand | 3.75 |
| Firm information capacity | 3.70 |
| Customer relationship management | 3.65 |
| Customer demand  satisfaction | 3.65 |
| Products portfolio | 3.65 |
| Cost control | 3.63 |
| R&D capabilities | 3.64 |
| Relationship with local government | 3.60 |
| Raw materials/parts procurement | 3.58 |
| Capital operation capabilities | 3.58 |
| Logistics | 3.49 |
| Control of distribution channels | 3.47 |

Note: 1 = very disadvantageous; 5 = very advantageous.

position a Chinese subsidiary is able to secure in the MNC network. As seen from Table 5.21, accumulation of firm competitive advantages is the most significant factor in the MNC network strategic position of MNC subsidiaries in China.

The significance of the MNC subsidiaries in the MNC network depends on their own experiences and the accumulation of core competences. Most of the respondents believe that subsidiaries' solid performance and growth and development goals are the most important factors that impact their positions within the network, while the parent company and the host country are less significant in this aspect.

## Hypothesis 5: competitive advantage

### Context

Quality control, firm image and quality of management team were perceived as the most significant factors for the competitive advantage of MNC subsidiaries in China (Table 5.22).

### Test of Hypotheses

**Hypothesis 5.1: the competitive advantage of MNC subsidiaries in China differ depending on the national origin of their parent company.**
The top three competitive advantage factors for MNC subsidiaries in China from different country origins are in Table 5.23. Quality control is among the top three for each of the nations.

Overall, there were no significant differences in competitive advantages for subsidiaries across different country origins (Table 5.24).

**Table 5.22** Significance of competitive advantage factors

| Serial No. | US | Japan | EU | Korea |
|---|---|---|---|---|
| 1 | Quality control | Quality control | Core technology | Competitive advantages within MNC network |
| 2 | The quality of management team | Firm image | Quality control | Quality of management team |
| 3 | Firm image | Brand | Function and price ratio for products | Quality control |

| Table 5.23 | Three most significant competitive advantage factors by country |

| Competitive advantage factor | Chi square value | df | p-value |
|---|---|---|---|
| Brand | 3.035 | 3 | 0.386 |
| Firm image | 2.309 | 3 | 0.511 |
| Product portfolio | 3.238 | 3 | 0.356 |
| Function and price ratio for products | 1.228 | 3 | 0.746 |
| Service | 1.339 | 3 | 0.720 |
| Control over distribution channels | 6.684 | 3 | 0.083 |
| Customer demand satisfaction | 0.228 | 3 | 0.973 |
| Customer relationship management | 0.482 | 3 | 0.923 |
| Raw materials/parts procurement | 1.433 | 3 | 0.698 |
| Cost control | 0.490 | 3 | 0.921 |
| Quality control | 1.248 | 3 | 0.741 |
| Logistics | 4.284 | 3 | 0.232 |
| Core technology | 4.500 | 3 | 0.212 |
| R&D capabilities | 4.274 | 3 | 0.233 |
| Quality of the management team | 0.803 | 3 | 0.849 |
| Firm information capacity | 0.545 | 3 | 0.909 |
| Capital operation capabilities | 2.405 | 3 | 0.493 |
| Competitive advantages within MNC network | 5.345 | 3 | 0.148 |
| Relations with local government | 1.921 | 3 | 0.589 |

| Table 5.24 | Comparison of competitive edge of different country MNC subsidiaries in China |

| | Different country | | | | Variance test | Mean differences | | |
|---|---|---|---|---|---|---|---|---|
| | US | Japan | EU | Korea | P value | T stat. value | df | P value |
| Distribution channels control | 3.64 | | | 2.95 | 0.814 | 2.237 | 41 | 0.025 |
| | | 3.69 | | 2.95 | 0.681 | 2.106 | 32 | 0.043 |
| Internal advantages of parent network | 4.24 | | | 3.45 | 0.815 | −2.147 | 33 | 0.039 |

| Table 5.25 | Selected competitive advantage factors by country | | | |

| Order | Chemical pharmaceutical | Mechanical engineering | Electrical and electronic equipment | Light textile |
|---|---|---|---|---|
| 1 | R&D capability | R&D capability | Quality of management team | Service |
| 2 | Core technology | Core technology | Business image | Firm image |
| 3 | Quality management | Quality management | Competitive advantages within MNC network | Quality management |

More specific analysis in Table 5.25 indicated that the MNC subsidiaries from the US and Japan have more advantages than South Korea subsidiaries in control over distribution channels. The parent network of US subsidiaries has stronger internal advantages than that of South Korean subsidiaries. South Korean subsidiaries in China are comparatively younger, with an average age of 6.88 years. Most are situated only in the Bohai Economic Zone and have much weaker distribution channels.

**Hypothesis 5.2: competitive advantages of MNC subsidiaries in China differ depending on their industry of operation.**
The top three competitive advantage factors for MNC subsidiaries in China from different industries are in Table 5.26. Quality control, followed by R&D capability and core technology appear as significant factors.

The Kruskal-Wallis test shows that none of the competitive advantage factors vary across industries (Table 5.27).

**Hypothesis 5.3: competitive advantages of MNC subsidiaries in China differ depending on their relative market share.**

Service, distribution channel control, customer demand satisfaction, logistics, R&D capabilities and information capacity variables show significant differences across MNC subsidiaries in China with varying relative market shares – i.e. ratio of the firm's market share and the market share of a dominant competitor (Table 5.28).

**Table 5.26** Three most significant competitive advantage factors by industry

| Comparative advantage | Chi square value | Degree of freedom | Significance |
|---|---|---|---|
| Brand | 14.19277 | 14 | 0.435450 |
| Firm image | 13.48806 | 14 | 0.488504 |
| Product portfolio | 15.23082 | 12 | 0.229056 |
| Function and price ratio for products | 3.831775 | 13 | 0.992853 |
| Service | 7.317902 | 12 | 0.835910 |
| Control of distribution channels | 6.663543 | 12 | 0.879024 |
| Customer demand satisfaction | 14.54333 | 12 | 0.267365 |
| Customer relationship management | 8.715514 | 13 | 0.794074 |
| Raw materials/parts procurement | 14.35199 | 12 | 0.278798 |
| Cost control | 6.973348 | 12 | 0.859370 |
| Quality control | 19.75731 | 13 | 0.101429 |
| Logistics | 7.928436 | 12 | 0.790698 |
| Core technology | 15.65446 | 12 | 0.207580 |
| R&D ability | 22.10903 | 13 | 0.053695 |
| Quality of the management team | 12.35941 | 13 | 0.498415 |
| Firm information capacity | 7.332576 | 12 | 0.834876 |
| Capital operation capabilities | 10.54298 | 12 | 0.568437 |
| Competitive advantages within MNC network | 14.58427 | 12 | 0.264962 |
| Relations with local government | 12.07708 | 13 | 0.521334 |

| Table 5.27 | Competitive advantage factors by industry, Kruskal-Wallis test | | |

| Comparative advantage factors | Chi-square value | df | p-value |
|---|---|---|---|
| Brand | 3.316 | 4 | 0.506 |
| Firm image | 9.218 | 4 | 0.056 |
| Product portfolio | 9.181 | 4 | 0.057 |
| Function and price ratio for products | 6.449 | 4 | 0.168 |
| Service | 13.786 | 4 | **0.008 |
| Control the distribution channels | 11.101 | 4 | **0.025 |
| Customer demand satisfaction | 12.254 | 4 | **0.016 |
| Customer relationship management | 8.922 | 4 | 0.063 |
| Raw materials/parts procurement | 4.137 | 4 | 0.388 |
| Cost control | 2.386 | 4 | 0.665 |
| Quality control | 6.312 | 4 | 0.177 |
| Logistics | 11.696 | 4 | *0.020 |
| Core technology | 9.047 | 4 | 0.060 |
| R&D capability | 15.118 | 4 | **0.004 |
| Quality of the management team | 8.218 | 4 | 0.084 |
| Firm information capacity | 10.797 | 4 | **0.029 |
| Capital operation capabilities | 5.884 | 4 | 0.208 |
| Competitive advantages within MNC network | 2.279 | 4 | 0.685 |
| Relations with local government | 6.949 | 4 | 0.139 |

Note: ** statistically significant with $\alpha = 0.05$ (two-tail test).

All the competitive advantage factors are rated higher for the MNC subsidiaries whose relative market share from a dominant competitor is more than 1.5 times (Table 5.28).

We also conducted comparison tests on subsidiaries with relative market shares of more than 1 versus less than 1 (Table 5.29). Subsidiaries with a stronger competitive position report stronger competitive advantages in product, service, customer relation, quality, logistics, core technology and R&D capability.

**Table 5.28** Competitive advantage factors by relative market share, Kruskal-Wallis test

| Competitive advantages | Relative market shares | | | | |
|---|---|---|---|---|---|
| | >1.5 | 1.0-1.5 | equal | 0.5-1.0 | <0.5 |
| Brand | 4.33 (1.211) | 3.77 (0.832) | 3.60 (0.548) | 3.72 (0.752) | 3.83 (1.169) |
| Firm image | 4.67 (0.516) | 3.83 (0.835) | 3.50 (0.577) | 3.71 (0.686) | 4.17 (0.753) |
| Product portfolio | 4.17 (0.753) | 3.92 (0.793) | 3.20 (0.447) | 3.41 (0.712) | 3.00 (1.265) |
| Function and price ratio for products | 4.17 (0.983) | 3.92 (0.900) | 3.80 (0.837) | 3.50 (0.516) | 2.80 (1.095) |
| Service | 4.67 (0.516) | 4.00 (0.707) | 3.50 (0.577) | 3.47 (0.717) | 3.25 (0.500) |
| Control over distribution channels | 4.60 (0.548) | 3.58 (0.900) | 3.50 (0.577) | 3.06 (0.929) | 3.25 (0.500) |
| Customer demand satisfaction | 4.60 (0.548) | 3.50 (0.674) | 3.50 (0.577) | 3.78 (0.732) | 2.60 (1.140) |
| Customer relationship management | 4.40 (0.894) | 3.67 (0.778) | 3.25 (0.500) | 3.40 (0.737) | 3.00 (0.000) |
| Raw materials/parts procurement | 4.25 (0.957) | 3.67 (0.651) | 3.25 (0.500) | 3.40 (0.986) | 3.50 (0.837) |
| Cost control | 4.25 (0.957) | 3.54 (0.776) | 3.60 (0.894) | 3.53 (0.717) | 3.33 (1.366) |
| Quality control | 4.67 (0.516) | 4.08 (0.793) | 3.80 (1.095) | 3.69 (1.014) | 3.67 (0.816) |
| Logistics | 4.40 (0.894) | 3.64 (0.674) | 3.25 (0.500) | 3.00 (0.632) | 3.50 (0.577) |
| Core technology | 4.17 (0.983) | 4.00 (0.632) | 3.50 (1.000) | 3.25 (0.683) | 3.50 (1.000) |
| R&D capability | 4.00 (0.894) | 3.92 (0.669) | 3.33 (0.577) | 3.06 (0.772) | 2.40 (0.894) |
| Quality of management team | 4.40 (0.548) | 3.60 (0.699) | 3.00 (0.000) | 3.75 (0.683) | 3.40 (1.140) |
| Firm information capacity | 4.67 (0.516) | 4.00 (0.775) | 3.33 (0.577) | 3.53 (0.834) | 3.20 (1.095) |
| Capital operation capabilities | 4.50 (1.000) | 3.55 (0.522) | 3.00 (0.000) | 3.50 (0.894) | 3.20 (1.304) |
| Competitive advantages within MNC network | 4.25 (0.957) | 3.82 (0.751) | 3.75 (0.957) | 3.69 (0.704) | 3.40 (1.140) |
| Relations with local government | 4.40 (0.894) | 3.50 (0.798) | 3.25 (0.500) | 3.25 (0.856) | 3.00 (1.000) |

Note: The data in the table are means and the figures in brackets are sample standard deviation.

**Table 5.29** Competitive advantage factors – mean differences based on relative market share

| | Relative market share | | Variance test | | Mean differences | |
|---|---|---|---|---|---|---|
| | >1 | <1 | p-value | T-value | df | p-value |
| Product portfolio | 4.00 | 3.30 | 0.550 | 2.66 | 39 | 0.011 |
| Service | 4.21 | 3.43 | 0.976 | 3.56 | 38 | 0.001 |
| Control of distribution channels | 3.88 | 3.10 | 0.335 | 2.67 | 35 | 0.011 |
| Customer relations management | 3.88 | 3.32 | 0.531 | 2.22 | 34 | 0.033 |
| Quality control | 4.28 | 3.68 | 0.530 | 2.17 | 38 | 0.036 |
| Logistics | 3.88 | 3.10 | 0.172 | 3.22 | 34 | 0.003 |
| Core technology | 4.06 | 3.30 | 0.982 | 3.11 | 35 | 0.004 |
| R&D capability | 3.94 | 2.90 | 0.954 | 4.13 | 37 | 0.001 |

**Hypothesis 5.4: competitive advantages of MNC subsidiaries in China differ depending on their perceived SWOT.**

Means on the competitive advantage factors for the three SWOT clusters are given in Table 5.30. The SO subsidiaries enjoy the strongest competitive advantages in all categories, followed by ST subsidiaries, while WO subsidiaries have the weakest competitive advantages. When subsidiaries have strong internal resources and capabilities, they will have better positions even when faced with market environment threats. Conversely, WO subsidiaries cannot make the best use of possible market opportunities because they lack core competencies to establish strong competitive advantages. Overall, all three types of subsidiaries have mean scores of more than 3 in branding, corporate image, product portfolio, services, distribution channels control and parenting advantage. All of these subsidiaries have established a very strong competitive base through years of operations in China.

| Table 5.30 | Competitive advantage factors by perceived SWOT posture |

| Competitive advantages | ST | | SO | | WO | |
|---|---|---|---|---|---|---|
| | Mean | Standard deviation | Mean | Standard deviation | Mean | Standard deviation |
| Branding | 3.43 | 0.746 | 3.96 | 0.824 | 3.32 | 1.057 |
| Firm image | 3.68 | 0.671 | 4.13 | 0.815 | 3.44 | 0.922 |
| Product portfolio | 3.57 | 0.811 | 3.93 | 0.772 | 2.94 | 0.998 |
| Service | 3.76 | 0.752 | 4.07 | 0.768 | 3.24 | 0.903 |
| Distribution channels control | 3.06 | 0.827 | 3.75 | 0.927 | 3.07 | 0.961 |
| Quality control | 3.94 | 0.929 | 4.13 | 0.718 | 3.38 | 0.957 |
| Parent network internal advantages | 3.43 | 0.646 | 3.98 | 0.832 | 3.36 | 0.745 |

## Hypothesis 6: competitive advantage initiatives

Table 5.31 shows that all the competitive advantage factors vary significantly across the three SWOT clusters.

**Hypothesis 6.1: competitive advantage initiatives of MNC subsidiaries in China differ depending on the national origin of their parent company.**

### Context

Table 5.32 shows that MNC subsidiaries in China perceive firm image, quality control, brand, service and cost control as the most significant initiatives for enhancing their competitive advantage, with means of more than 4.0, and at least 70 per cent respondents identifying as significant.

**Table 5.31**  Competitive advantage factors by perceived SWOT posture, ANOVA

| Competitive advantages | | Variation | df | Mean variation | F value | Homogeneous variance | p-value |
|---|---|---|---|---|---|---|---|
| Branding | Group | 7.551 | 2 | 3.776 | 5.081 | 0.925 | 0.008 |
| | In group | 63.165 | 85 | 0.743 | | | |
| | Total | 70.716 | 87 | | | | |
| Firm image | Group | 7.024 | 2 | 3.512 | 5.353 | 0.491 | 0.007 |
| | In group | 53.800 | 82 | 0.656 | | | |
| | Total | 60.824 | 84 | | | | |
| Product portfolio | Group | 11.983 | 2 | 5.991 | 8.733 | 0.357 | 0.0001 |
| | In group | 54.885 | 80 | 0.686 | | | |
| | Total | 66.867 | 82 | | | | |
| Service | Group | 8.546 | 2 | 4.273 | 6.741 | 0.073 | 0.002 |
| | In group | 46.908 | 74 | 0.634 | | | |
| | Total | 55.455 | 76 | | | | |
| Distribution channels control | Group | 8.403 | 2 | 4.202 | 5.053 | 2.086 | 0.009 |
| | In group | 57.375 | 69 | 0.832 | | | |
| | Total | 65.778 | 71 | | | | |
| Quality management | Group | 6.775 | 2 | 3.387 | 5.091 | 0.824 | 0.008 |
| | In group | 49.905 | 75 | 0.665 | | | |
| | Total | 56.679 | 77 | | | | |
| Parent network internal advantages | Group | 5.617 | 2 | 2.809 | 4.608 | 0.452 | 0.013 |
| | In group | 39.618 | 65 | 0.610 | | | |
| | Total | 45.235 | 67 | | | | |

**Table 5.32**   Competitive advantage initiatives, statistics

| Competitive advantage initiatives | Mean | % reporting significant (rating of 4 and 5) |
|---|---|---|
| Firm image | 4.25 | 82.81% |
| Quality control | 4.16 | 71.88% |
| Brand | 4.16 | 78.13% |
| Service | 4.13 | 72.66% |
| Cost control | 4.12 | 70.31% |
| Customer relation management | 4.09 | 60.94% |
| Quality of management team | 4.07 | 68.75% |
| Customer demand satisfaction | 4.06 | 64.84% |
| Function and price ratio for products | 4.03 | 69.53% |
| R&D capability | 4.00 | 68.75% |
| Control over distribution channels | 3.99 | 65.63% |
| Core technology | 3.96 | 66.41% |
| Competitive advantages within MNC network | 3.94 | 61.72% |
| Firm information capacity | 3.95 | 65.63% |
| Relationship with local government | 3.94 | 60.94% |
| Capital operation capabilities | 3.88 | 65.63% |
| Logistics | 3.88 | 65.63% |
| Product portfolio | 3.87 | 69.53% |
| Raw materials/parts procurement | 3.86 | 70.31% |

Note: Composite percentage is the sum of the competitive advantage effective percentages for options 4 and 5 (significant and very significant); 1 = very insignificant; 5 = very significant.

## Test of hypotheses

**Hypothesis 6.1: competitive advantage initiatives of MNC subsidiaries in China differ depending on the national origin of their parent company.**

The Kruskal-Wallis test showed that none of the competitive advantage initiatives of the MNC subsidiaries in China vary

| Table 5.33 | Three most significant competitive advantage initiatives by country |
|---|---|

| No. | US | Japan | EU | Korea |
|---|---|---|---|---|
| 1 | Firm image | Function and price ratio for products | Quality control | Firm image |
| 2 | Quality of management team | Brand | Relationship with local government | Quality control |
| 3 | Customer relation management | Service | Cost control | Customer relation management |

by country origins (p > 0.05). The top three initiatives for each country origin are given in Table 5.33. Business image, customer relations management and quality control all appeared twice among four origins.

More specific analysis in Table 5.34 shows that US MNC subsidiaries are more inclined to build their competitive advantages through management team quality and relationship with local government.

| Table 5.34 | Competitive advantage initiatives by country, ANOVA |
|---|---|

| | National origin | | | | Variance test | | Significance of mean differences | |
|---|---|---|---|---|---|---|---|---|
| | US | Japan | EU | South Korea | p-value | T-value | df | p-value |
| Quality of management team | 4.28 | | 3.69 | | 0.598 | 2.554 | 39 | 0.015 |
| Relations with local government | 4.13 | | | 3.42 | 0.612 | 2.343 | 41 | 0.024 |
| | | | 4.14 | 3.42 | 0.700 | 2.006 | 31 | 0.050 |

**Hypothesis 6.2: competitive advantage initiatives of MNC subsidiaries in China differ depending on their industry of operation.**

The Kruskal-Wallis test showed that none of the competitive advantage initiatives vary by industry. The top three means for major industries are given in Table 5.35. Firm image and customer relationship management are the two leading competitive advantage initiatives in these industries.

To dig deeper, we selected three industries with larger sample sizes (Table 5.36). Subsidiaries in the chemical/pharmaceutical industry report significantly greater competitive advantage in product portfolio, quality management, R&D capability and local government relations, compared with those in the electronic/electrical and light industries. In the chemical/pharmaceutical industry, the emphasis is on innovative high-tech products driven by R&D, economies of scale and strict quality control. These subsidiaries are usually situated near the production facilities

**Table 5.35**    Three most significant competitive advantage initiatives by industry

| Order | Chemical/ pharmaceutical | Mechanical engineering | Electrical and electronic equipment | Light/textile |
|---|---|---|---|---|
| 1 | Brand | Customer relation management | Quality control | Firm information capacity |
| 2 | Firm image | Firm image | Firm image | Function and price ratio for products |
| 3 | Capital operation capabilities | R&D ability | Customer relation management | Cost control |

| Table 5.36 | Competitive advantage initiatives by industry, mean difference test |

| | Mean scores | | | Variance test | | Mean differences | |
|---|---|---|---|---|---|---|---|
| | Chemical/ pharma-ceutical industry | Electronic/ electrical equipment industry | Light industry/ textile industry | p-value | t-value | df | p-value |
| Product portfolio advantages | 4.09 | | 3.28 | 0.575 | 2.23 | 27 | 0.034 |
| Quality management advantages | 4.50 | 3.57 | | 0.296 | 2.69 | 31 | 0.011 |
| R&D capability advantages | 4.17 | 3.41 | | 0.366 | 2.49 | 32 | 0.018 |
| | 4.17 | | 3.31 | 0.563 | 2.61 | 26 | 0.015 |
| Relations with local government | 4.10 | | 3.50 | 0.837 | 2.11 | 22 | 0.047 |

of raw materials, and because of this geographical orientation, they have a closer relationship with the local governments.

**Hypothesis 6.3: competitive advantage initiatives of MNC subsidiaries in China differ depending on their relative market share.**

The Kruskal-Wallis test showed that none of the competitive advantage initiatives vary in their significance across firms with different relative market shares (Table 5.37). Yet, each of the competitive advantage initiatives is rated to be more significant by the firms with positive relative market shares, as can be seen below. The different is especially large for relationship management with customers and with local government.

| Table 5.37 | Competitive advantage initiatives by relative market share |
| | |

| Means to enhance competitive advantages | Relative market shares >1 | Relative market shares <1 | Mean difference |
|---|---|---|---|
| Customer relation management | 4.29 | 3.48 | 0.81 |
| Relationship with local government | 4.13 | 3.53 | 0.60 |
| Core technology | 4.14 | 3.63 | 0.51 |
| Service | 4.53 | 4.07 | 0.45 |
| Customer demand satisfaction | 4.25 | 3.79 | 0.45 |
| Quality control | 4.43 | 4.03 | 0.39 |
| Quality of management team | 4.25 | 3.86 | 0.39 |
| Control the distribution channels | 4.28 | 3.90 | 0.38 |
| Competitive advantages within MNC network | 3.92 | 3.55 | 0.37 |
| Firm information capacity | 4.16 | 3.82 | 0.34 |
| Capital operation capabilities | 4.03 | 3.73 | 0.31 |
| Product portfolio | 4.26 | 4.00 | 0.26 |
| R&D ability | 4.04 | 3.78 | 0.26 |
| Brand | 4.38 | 4.13 | 0.24 |
| Logistics | 3.96 | 3.74 | 0.22 |
| Raw materials/ parts procurement | 4.04 | 3.83 | 0.21 |
| Cost control | 4.39 | 4.20 | 0.19 |
| Function and price ratio for products | 4.33 | 4.13 | 0.19 |
| Firm image | 4.44 | 4.26 | 0.18 |

Note: 1 = very insignificant; 5 = very significant.

| Table 5.38 | | Selected competitive advantage initiatives by perceived SWOT posture, statistics | | | | |
|---|---|---|---|---|---|---|

| Variable | ST | | SO | | WO | |
|---|---|---|---|---|---|---|
| | Mean | Standard deviation | Mean | Standard deviation | Mean | Standard deviation |
| Corporate image | 4.26 | 0.619 | 4.40 | 0.689 | 3.90 | 0.852 |
| Product portfolio | 4.00 | 0.649 | 4.09 | 0.684 | 3.00 | 1.155 |

Note: ST = strength–threat, SO = strength–opportunity, WO = weakness–opportunity.

## Hypothesis 6.4: competitive advantage initiatives of MNC subsidiaries in China differ depending on their perceived SWOT.

Table 5.38 gives mean scores on competitive advantage initiatives across the perceived SWOT clusters. ANOVA revealed that the three types of MNC subsidiaries in China differ significantly in corporate image and product portfolio initiatives (Table 5.39). Other factors were not significant.

MNC subsidiaries in the SO cluster put higher priority on corporate image and product portfolio initiatives than do the subsidiaries, while those in the WO cluster put least priority. Subsidiaries with internal strengths and capabilities plan to invest more on corporate image and product portfolio

| Table 5.39 | | Selected competitive advantage initiatives by perceived SWOT posture, ANOVA | | | | | |
|---|---|---|---|---|---|---|---|

| Variable | | Variation | Freedom | Mean variation | F value | Homogeneous variance | p-value |
|---|---|---|---|---|---|---|---|
| Business image | Group | 3.576 | 2 | 1.788 | 3.544 | 0.591 | 0.033 |
| | In group | 46.914 | 93 | 0.504 | | | |
| | Total | 50.490 | 95 | | | | |
| Product portfolio | Group | 14.549 | 2 | 7.275 | 11.608 | 1.769 | 0.001 |
| | In group | 47.628 | 76 | 0.627 | | | |
| | Total | 62.177 | 78 | | | | |

| Table 5.40 | Selected competitive advantage initiatives by perceived SWOT posture, mean differences test | | | |
|---|---|---|---|---|

| Variable | Comparing groups | Difference | Significant levels | Sorting groups |
|---|---|---|---|---|
| Corporate image | SO-ST | 0.14 | | SO > ST > WO |
| | ST-WO | −0.36 | * | |
| | SO-WO | 0.50 | ** | |
| Product portfolio | SO-ST | 0.09 | | SO > ST > WO |
| | ST-WO | 1.00 | ** | |
| | SO-WO | 1.09 | ** | |

Note: $**p < 0.05$; $*p < 0.01$.

initiatives, both to capitalise on the favourable market environment as well as to respond to external threats. Conversely, the WO subsidiaries do not have the internal capabilities to utilise the opportunities. Overall, the mean scores for each of the three clusters of subsidiaries exceed 3, indicating that all are aware of the significance of corporate image and product portfolio initiatives.

Table 5.41 and Figure 5.3 compare competitive advantage initiatives for the current stage and for the future phase based on the findings for Hypotheses 5.4 and 6.4. ST subsidiaries currently have a greater advantage in quality management and will shift their strategic focus in future to firm image and customer relations. These new priorities are in response to the threats arising from the changing market environment and will help attract new customers and strategic partners and increase business development opportunities. SO subsidiaries currently have a greater advantage in firm image and quality management and plan to focus on firm image and branding in future. The shift from quality to branding will help SO subsidiaries take pre-emptive actions to maintain their leadership position for the future. WO subsidiaries currently have a greater advantage in raw materials and parts procurement and management team quality, but plan

| Table 5.41 | Competitive advantage factors and initiatives by perceived SWOT posture | | |
|---|---|---|---|

| Phases | OT subsidiaries | SO subsidiaries | WO subsidiaries |
|---|---|---|---|
| Advantages at current stage | Quality control | Corporate image; Quality control | Raw materials/parts; Procurement; Management team quality |
| Strategic initiatives for future phase | Corporate image; Customer relationship management | Corporate image; Branding | Quality control; Branding; Distribution channels control |

to shift attention to quality management, branding and distribution channels control. The strategic priority for these firms is to create and cultivate their unique core competences to better seize market opportunities. That requires catching up with industry benchmarks in strengthening quality management, branding management and control of distribution channels.

| Figure 5.3 | Strategic trend |
|---|---|

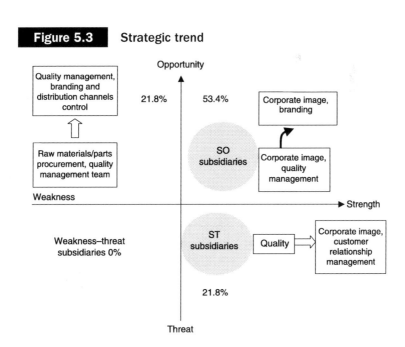

# Summary

Table 5.42 summarises the support for the strategic intent hypotheses in this study.

| Table 5.42 | Summary of results of strategic intent hypothesis testing |
| --- | --- |

| Hypotheses group | Hypotheses | Testing result |
| --- | --- | --- |
| 1 Investment mode | 1.1: The entry investment mode varies significantly across MNC subsidiaries in China, depending *on the national origin of their parent company.* | Substantiated |
| | 1.2: The entry investment mode varies significantly across MNC subsidiaries in China, depending *on the time of their entry in China.* | Substantiated |
| | 1.3: The present investment mode of MNC subsidiaries in China is significantly related to their industry market share. | Not substantiated |
| 2 Shareholding ratio | No hypothesis was advanced | |
| 3 Growth and development factors | No hypothesis was advanced | |
| 4 Competitive mandate | No hypothesis was advanced | |
| 5 Competitive advantages | 5.1: Competitive advantages of MNC subsidiaries in China differ depending *on the national origin of their parent company.* | Substantiated |
| | 5.2: Competitive advantages of MNC subsidiaries in China differ depending *on their industry of operation.* | Not substantiated |
| | 5.3: Competitive advantages of MNC subsidiaries in China differ depending *on their relative market share.* | Substantiated |
| | 5.4: Competitive advantages of MNC subsidiaries in China differ depending *on their perceived SWOT.* | Substantiated |

*(Continued)*

| Table 5.42 | Summary of results of strategic intent hypothesis testing *(continued)* |

| Hypotheses group | Hypotheses | Testing result |
|---|---|---|
| 6 Competitive advantage initiatives | 6.1: Competitive advantage initiatives of MNC subsidiaries in China differ depending *on the national origin of their parent company.* | Not substantiated |
| | 6.2: Competitive advantage initiatives of MNC subsidiaries in China differ depending *on their industry of operation.* | Not substantiated |
| | 6.3: Competitive advantage initiatives of MNC subsidiaries in China differ depending *on their relative market share.* | Not substantiated |
| | 6.4: Competitive advantage initiatives of MNC subsidiaries in China differ depending *on their perceived SWOT.* | Not substantiated |

# Note

1   Relative market share is the ratio between market share of the focal company and that of the major competitor.

# 6

# Corporate and functional strategies

**Abstract:** In this chapter, we investigate corporate and functional strategies of MNC subsidiaries in China, including relationships with the parent company and with other subsidiaries, integration and localisation, M&A and alliance strategy, financial strategy, marketing strategy, knowledge transfer strategy, human resources strategy, R&D strategy and strategic blunders. The findings and analysis are summarised in a table.

**Key words:** Corporate, functional, strategy, relationship, parent company, subsidiaries, integration, localisation, M&A, alliance, financial strategy, marketing strategy, knowledge transfer strategy, human resources strategy, R&D strategy, strategic blunders.

## Hypotheses

### Hypothesis 1: relationships with the parent company and with other subsidiaries

- 1.1: Strength of ties of MNC subsidiaries in China with the parent company varies significantly depending *on the time of their entry in China.*

- 1.2: Strength of ties of MNC subsidiaries in China with the MNC network vary significantly depending *on the national origin of the parent company.*

- 1.3: Strength of ties of MNC subsidiaries in China with the parent company varies significantly depending *on the location of the headquarters.*

Strength of ties of MNC subsidiaries in China with their parent company was measured on a five-point scale (5 = very loose, 1 = very close) on the items given in Table 6.1.

Location of the headquarters is measured using a categorical variable with ascending degree of localisation, with categories as global HQ, Asia-Pacific HQ, Greater China HQ and mainland China HQ.

## Hypothesis 2: integration and localisation

Respondents were asked about integration versus localisation pressures, and localisation in various functional strategies.

- 2.1: Integration and localisation pressures for MNC subsidiaries in China vary depending on their time of entry into China.

**Table 6.1**    Items to measure strength of ties

| |
|---|
| Finished product export ratio |
| Relationship quality between the parent firm and subsidiaries in organisational cultural management |
| Dependence on the parent company for technology |
| Dependence on the parent company for raw materials and spare parts supply |
| Dependence on the parent company for machinery and equipment import |
| Dependence on the parent company for sales channels |
| Implementation goodness of the parent company's decision in organisation designs and business processes |
| Dependence on the parent company for financing |
| Deployment of staff |
| Frequency of reporting to the parent company |

| Table 6.2 | Measuring integration and localisation pressures |

| Integration pressures | Localisation pressures |
|---|---|
| Emergence of transnational competitors | Raw material and energy access |
| Need for centralised investment | Customer demand preferences |
| Need for centralised technology | Distribution channel differences |
| Pressure for lowering costs | Replacement requirements and need for change |
| Need for universal use | Market structure adjustments |
| | Requests of the host government |

Integration and localisation pressures are measured on a five-point scale (1 = very low; 5 = very high), using the following items taken from the work of Doz and Prahalad (Table 6.2).

Functional strategy localisation is a single item measured on a five-point scale, for each of the functional areas separately (1 = very low; 5 = very high).

## Hypothesis 3: M&A and alliance strategy

Respondents were asked about the motives for M&As and for alliances by MNC subsidiaries in China. No specific hypothesis was advanced.

Motives for M&As and alliances were measured using multiple items on a five-point scale (1 = very insignificant; 5 = very significant).

## Hypothesis 4: financial strategy

- 4.1: Funding channels for MNC subsidiaries in China are significantly different, depending on if they are wholly versus majority foreign-owned.

| Table 6.3 | Items to measure funding channels |
|---|---|

| Parent funding |
|---|
| Local direct fundraising |
| Overseas direct fundraising |
| Overseas indirect fundraising |
| China funding |
| Local indirect fundraising |

- 4.2: Funding channels for MNC subsidiaries in China are significantly different, depending on the country of origin of their parent company.

- 4.3: Funding channels for MNC subsidiaries in China are significantly different, depending on their age.

Funding channels were measured using items given in Table 6.3 on a five-point scale (1 = very insignificant; 5 = very significant).

## Hypothesis 5: marketing strategy

- 5.1: The export–sales ratio of MNC subsidiaries in China varies significantly depending on the national origin of the parent companies.

- 5.2: The marketing decision-making autonomy varies significantly depending on the export ratio of MNC subsidiaries in China.

The marketing decision-making autonomy of MNC subsidiaries in China was measured using items on a five-point scale (1 = very insignificant; 5 = very significant).

## Hypothesis 6: knowledge transfer strategy

Respondents were asked about the importance of different methods of knowledge transfer between the parent company and MNC subsidiaries in China, and the factors influencing this knowledge transfer.

- 6.1: The avenues for knowledge flow from the parent MNC to the subsidiaries in China vary depending on their industry of operation.

The methods of knowledge transfer between the parent company and the Chinese subsidiaries, and the factors influencing this knowledge transfer, were each measured using multiple items measured on a five-point scale (1 = very insignificant; 5 = very significant).

## Hypothesis 7: human resources strategy

- 7.1: The autonomy in human resource management function varies across MNC subsidiaries in China depending on their country of origin.
- 7.2: The degree of labour confrontation faced by MNC subsidiaries in China varies significantly depending on their SWOT perception.

The degree of labour confrontation was measured using a single item on a five-point scale (1 = very low; 5 = very high).

## Hypothesis 8: R&D strategy

- 8.1: The innovation initiatives by MNC subsidiaries in China vary depending on their country of origin.
- 8.2: The innovation initiatives by MNC subsidiaries in China vary depending on their industry of operation.

Several variables related to R&D strategy were measured.

## Hypothesis 9: strategic blunders

Sources of strategic blunders were measured using multiple items measured on a five-point scale (1 = very unimportant; 5 = very important).

# Findings and analysis

## Hypothesis 1: subsidiaries' relationships

### Context

MNC subsidiaries in China reported their ties with the parent company to be the strongest in the area of frequent reporting to the parent company, followed by dependence for technology and for financing (Table 6.4).

**Table 6.4**    Strength of ties with parent, statistics

| Strength of ties with the parent company | N | Mean | Standard deviation |
|---|---|---|---|
| Frequency of reporting to the parent company | 91 | 4.00 | 0.882 |
| Dependence on the parent company for technology | 94 | 3.94 | 0.971 |
| Dependence on the parent company for financing | 95 | 3.91 | 0.935 |
| Dependence on the parent company for raw materials and spare parts supply | 97 | 3.72 | 0.997 |
| Relationship quality between the parent firm and subsidiaries in organisational cultural management | 99 | 3.66 | 0.847 |
| Dependence on the parent company for machinery and equipment import | 96 | 3.65 | 1.005 |
| Implementation goodness of the parent company's decision in organisation designs and business processes | 92 | 3.63 | 0.848 |
| Dependence on the parent company for sales channels | 94 | 3.51 | 1.105 |
| Finished product export ratio | 90 | 3.50 | 1.164 |
| Deployment of staff | 89 | 3.18 | 0.912 |

Note: 1 = very loose; 5 = very close.

| Table 6.5 | Strength of ties with parent by time of entry, Kruskal-Wallis test |

|  | Strategic autonomy variables |
| --- | --- |
| Chi square value | 11.332 |
| Degree of freedom | 18 |
| p-value | 0.880 |

## Test of hypotheses

**Hypothesis 1.1: strength of ties of MNC subsidiaries in China with the parent company vary significantly depending on the time of their entry in China.**
Strength of ties with the parent company does not vary with the time of entry into China (Table 6.5).

**Hypothesis 1.2: strength of ties of MNC subsidiaries in China with the MNC network vary significantly depending on the national origin of the parent company.**
The relationship of MNC subsidiaries with parent companies varies depending on the parent's national origin because of cultural and strategic factors. We conducted a chi square test on the strength of the tie with the parent company, across subsidiaries with different country origins (Table 6.6). The tie strength varies significantly across different national origins for two items – finished product export ratio and dependence on the parent company for sales channels.

We also conducted a chi square test on how the strength of ties with other subsidiaries varies across MNC subsidiaries of different national origins (Table 6.7). Different national subsidiaries vary in their relationship with other subsidiaries in terms of knowledge-sharing and flow.

Japanese parent companies have highly centralised control over their subsidiaries in China and knowledge exchange

**Table 6.6** Strength of ties with parent by country, chi square test

|  | Chi square value | df | p-value |
|---|---|---|---|
| Finished product export ratio | 15.638 | 3 | 0.001 |
| Relationship quality between the parent firm and subsidiaries in organisational cultural management | 2.564 | 3 | 0.464 |
| Dependence on parent company for technology | 1.624 | 3 | 0.654 |
| Dependence on the parent company for raw materials and spare parts supply | 5.524 | 3 | 0.137 |
| Dependence on the parent company for machinery and equipment import | 6.340 | 3 | 0.096 |
| Dependence on the parent company for sales channels | 19.635 | 3 | 0.001 |
| Implementation goodness of the parent company's decision in organisation designs and business processes | 1.080 | 3 | 0.782 |
| Dependence on the parent company for financing | 6.425 | 3 | 0.093 |
| Deployment of staff | 1.343 | 3 | 0.719 |
| Frequency of reporting to the parent company | 2.398 | 3 | 0.494 |

**Table 6.7** Strength of ties with other subsidiaries, chi square test

|  | Chi square value | df | p-value |
|---|---|---|---|
| Deployment of funds among subsidiaries | 1.568 | 3 | 0.667 |
| Deployment of staff among subsidiaries | 5.217 | 3 | 0.157 |
| Technical support and dependence | 1.787 | 3 | 0.618 |
| Raw materials and spare parts supply among subsidiaries | 6.291 | 3 | 0.098 |
| Communications frequencies among subsidiaries | 4.635 | 3 | 0.201 |
| Knowledge-sharing and flow | 9.960 | 3 | 0.019 |

between subsidiaries is very low. EU MNC parent companies have highly decentralised control on coordination mechanism over their subsidiaries in China and knowledge exchanges between subsidiaries are very high. US MNC parent companies stay in between the two regions on both counts.

**Hypothesis 1.3: strength of ties of MNC subsidiaries in China with the parent company vary significantly depending on the location of the headquarters.**

The mean scores for the strength of ties with the parent company are greatest under the global HQ model, implying that MNC subsidiaries in China are most dependent on their HQ when the MNC does not have a regional or local HQ (Table 6.8).

We also found that the overall index mean for the strength of ties between the parent and MNC subsidiaries in China was greater than the overall index mean for the strength of ties between MNC subsidiaries in China and other subsidiaries in the MNC network (Table 6.9). Thus, MNC subsidiaries in China tend to have stronger links with the headquarters than with the other subsidiaries around the world.

The relationship between the parent company and with other subsidiaries reflects the control and coordination mechanisms of the MNCs. For effective demarcation of responsibilities and powers between the parent company and its subsidiaries, MNCs need to have a good control and coordination mechanism in place. For different strategic needs, MNCs adopt different organisational structures. MNC subsidiaries maintain their relationship with the parent company in frequency of reporting, technology and financing dependence, while keeping their relationship with other subsidiaries via sharing of knowledge and mutual communications.

**Table 6.8** Strength of ties with parent by HQ location, statistics

|  | Global headquarters | Asian-Pacific headquarters | Greater China headquarters | China headquarters |
|---|---|---|---|---|
| Finished product export ratio | 3.39 | 3.56 | 2.50 | 3.39 |
| Relationship quality between the parent firm and subsidiaries in organisational cultural management | 3.61 | 3.63 | 3.50 | 3.74 |
| Dependence on the parent company for technology | 4.24 | 4.00 | 3.25 | 3.64 |
| Dependence on the parent company for raw materials and spare parts supply | 3.57 | 3.80 | 4.00 | 3.77 |
| Dependence on the parent company for machinery and equipment import | 3.65 | 3.75 | 3.50 | 3.40 |
| Dependence on the parent company for sales channels | 3.40 | 3.68 | 2.50 | 3.33 |
| Implementation goodness of the parent company's decision in organisation designs and business processes | 3.57 | 3.50 | 3.83 | 3.72 |
| Dependence on the parent company for financing | 3.88 | 4.06 | 3.40 | 3.92 |
| Deployment of staff | 3.55 | 3.31 | 3.50 | 2.92 |
| Frequency of reporting to the parent company | 4.04 | 3.79 | 4.00 | 3.96 |

Note: 1 = very loose; 5 = very close.

| Table 6.9 | Strength of ties with parent and other subsidiaries, statistics | | |

| Strength of ties between the parent and subsidiaries | Mean | Strength of ties among subsidiaries | Mean |
|---|---|---|---|
| Finished product export ratio | 3.50 | Deployment of funds among subsidiaries | 3.06 |
| Relationship quality between the parent firm and subsidiaries in organisational cultural management | 3.66 | Deployment of staff among subsidiaries | 2.99 |
| Dependence on the parent company for technology | 3.94 | Technical support and dependence | 3.35 |
| Dependence on the parent company for raw materials and spare parts supply | 3.72 | Raw materials and spare parts supply among subsidiaries | 3.30 |
| Dependence on the parent company for machinery and equipment import | 3.65 | Communications frequencies among subsidiaries | 3.40 |
| Dependence on the parent company for sales channels | 3.51 | Knowledge-sharing and flow | 3.70 |
| Implementation goodness of the parent company's decision in organisation designs and business processes | 3.63 | | |
| Dependence on the parent company for financing | 3.91 | | |
| Deployment of staff | 3.18 | | |
| Communication frequencies among subsidiaries | 4.00 | | |
| **Overall index mean** | **3.67** | **Overall index mean** | **3.30** |

# Hypothesis 2: integration and localisation

## Context

A series of appropriate strategic actions for integration–localisation balance determine firms' final competitive advantages. Many MNCs have the economic capabilities and technical know-how to implement their global integration

**Table 6.10**   Integration and localisation, statistics

| Integration factors | Mean | Localisation factors | Mean |
|---|---|---|---|
| Emergence of transnational competitors | 3.61 | Differences in customer demand | 3.74 |
| Centralised need for investment | 3.24 | Differences in distribution channels | 3.49 |
| Centralised need for technology | 3.34 | Localisation need for product/service | 3.57 |
| Pressure for cutting down costs | 3.93 | Market structure adjustment | 3.64 |
| Need for standardisation in product and service | 3.62 | Demand of host government | 3.33 |
| Procurement for raw material and energy | 3.65 | | |
| **Overall index for integration pressures** | **3.58** | **Overall index for localisation pressures** | **3.56** |

Note: 1 = very insignificant; 5 = very significant.

strategies to reduce costs, but owing to the economic constraints (the market structure and consumer demand), political constraints (legal policy and government regulations) and intense competition in the Chinese market, they have to enhance their investments and efforts for localisation in production, talent, market channels and brand image. Findings suggested that the overall indices for integration pressures and for localisation pressures faced by MNC subsidiaries in China are about the same (Table 6.10).

## Integration–localisation by function

Localisation in the human resource function and marketing functions had a mean of more than 3.50, and more than 50 per cent of the respondents deemed it significant (Table 6.11). On the other hand, localisation in R&D and investment management strategy was relatively low. Thus, in important strategic functions of research and development strategies

| Table 6.11 | Localisation of various functional strategies, statistics |

| Function strategy | Samples | Mean | Standard deviation | % reporting localisation to be high or very high |
|---|---|---|---|---|
| HR localisation strategy | 99 | 3.68 | 0.946 | 62.7% |
| Marketing localisation strategy | 101 | 3.56 | 1.090 | 58.4% |
| R&D localisation strategy | 92 | 3.20 | 1.019 | 39.1% |
| Investment management localisation strategy | 85 | 3.06 | 0.956 | 34.2% |

Note: 1 = very low; 5 = very high for localisation.

and investment strategy, there exists a strong centralised trend, where the power of subsidiaries is limited. These subsidiaries are expected to be consistent with the requirements and expectations of the parent company.

Overall localisation pressures faced by MNC subsidiaries in China were significantly correlated with the localisation of each of their functional strategies – HR, marketing, R&D and investment management (Table 6.12).

## Test of hypothesis

**Hypothesis 2.1: integration and localisation pressures for MNC subsidiaries in China vary depending on the time of entry into China.**

The Kruskal-Wallis test shows only one significant coefficient: the localisation pressure for market structure adjustment (Table 6.13). In the formative stages of market entry in China, MNCs had few international competitors and experienced low industry concentration and low entry barriers. Using their brand products, technology, capital and other advantages, they rapidly beat domestic competitors and

| Table 6.12 | Localisation of various functional strategies by overall localisation pressure, correlation |
|---|---|

|  |  | Overall localisation pressures on the MNC subsidiary |
|---|---|---|
| HR strategy localisation | Pearson correlation | 0.252 |
|  | p-value (2 tails) | 0.007 |
|  | N | 88 |
| Market strategy localisation | Pearson correlation | 0.273 |
|  | p-value (2 tails) | 0.002 |
|  | N | 95 |
| R&D strategy localisation | Pearson correlation | 0.469 |
|  | p-value (2 tails) | 0.000 |
|  | N | 84 |
| Investment strategy localisation | Pearson correlation | 0.276 |
|  | p-value (2 tails) | 0.003 |
|  | N | 82 |

became market leaders. They created monopolist control by expanding market share and erecting entry barriers in their industries. For the later entrants, the market structure changed to a high degree of market concentration. Their competitors were no longer Chinese local firms but powerful MNC subsidiaries from the US or Europe. Because the market access barriers were now much higher, the late entrants could not gain competitive edge using the same strategy since the competitive advantages turned into competitive minimum requirements to stay in the game. Therefore many late entrants took the balanced approach of integration and localisation for more effective competition.

| **Table 6.13** | Integration and localisation pressures by time of entry |

|  | Chi square | df | p-value |
|---|---|---|---|
| Emergence of transnational competitors | 16.84 | 19 | 0.601 |
| Centralised need for investment | 20.38 | 18 | 0.312 |
| Centralised need for technology | 23.02 | 19 | 0.236 |
| Pressure for cutting down costs | 21.51 | 19 | 0.309 |
| Need for standardisation in product and service | 13.13 | 19 | 0.832 |
| Procurement for raw material and energy | 21.75 | 19 | 0.297 |
| Differences in customer demand | 17.93 | 19 | 0.527 |
| Differences in distribution channels | 11.03 | 19 | 0.923 |
| Localisation need for product/service | 17.65 | 19 | 0.546 |
| Market structure adjustment | 32.91 | 19 | 0.025 |
| Demand of host government | 26.29 | 18 | 0.093 |

Note: 1 = very low; 5 = very high for localisation.

## Hypothesis 3: M&A and alliance strategy

### Context

The question in the questionnaire is, 'In recent years, your subsidiary has merged with or acquired what types of enterprises in China?' There were 90 usable samples, among which 59 firms have not taken any actions in mergers and

| **Figure 6.1** | Integration and localisation indices by time of entry |

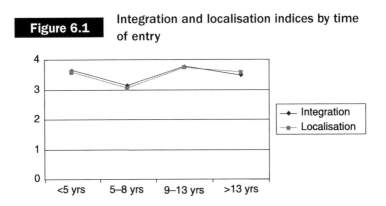

151

acquisition; two firms have acquired collective firms (state-owned in nature) and eight have acquired private firms; ten firms have acquired foreign-owned enterprises and three firms have acquired listed companies.

Thus, MNCs did not favour merger with or acquisition of local firms for their expansion. The reasons behind this were: (1) the Chinese government policy concerning foreign acquisition remained unclear and not transparent; (2) local protectionism is serious with complicated procedures and documentation; (3) there were government restrictions on some industries and on the proportion of equity holding; and (4) the overall quality and capabilities of domestic firms was relatively weak and M&A activities were not able to complement the MNC growth strategy and add value to MNC subsidiary core competences.

## Motives for M&As

Local productivity enhancement and shortening time to enter the Chinese market are the two most important motives for M&As by MNC subsidiaries in China, with more than 50 per cent of the respondents identifying these two to be significant, and means of more than 3.0. Knowledge access, management personnel access or funding access are not identified as significant by any of the respondents (Table 6.14).

## Motives for strategic alliances

Procurement cost reduction is the most significant motive for alliances by MNC subsidiaries in China, with more than 75 per cent of respondents rating that as significant, and with a mean of more than 3.50. Risk dispersion and joint R&D efforts or knowledge-sharing are the least significant motives (Table 6.15).

**Table 6.14**    Motives for mergers and acquisitions

| M&A motive | Sample size | Mean | Standard deviation | % reporting 4 or 5, on a 5-point scale |
|---|---|---|---|---|
| Enhance local productivity | 14 | 3.71 | 0.611 | 64.2 |
| Shorten cycle time to enter China market | 18 | 3.33 | 1.328 | 55.6 |
| Possession and use of brand name and resources of the acquired firm | 13 | 3.00 | 1.291 | 30.8 |
| Possess local distribution channels | 13 | 3.00 | 0.913 | 30.8 |
| Increase product lines | 12 | 2.92 | 1.084 | 33.3 |
| Buy cheap firm assets | 15 | 2.87 | 1.187 | 26.7 |
| Purchase special assets from the acquired firm | 15 | 2.87 | 1.125 | 26.7 |
| Lower procurement costs for raw materials and parts | 12 | 2.83 | 1.030 | 25.0 |
| Possess the technology of the acquired firm | 12 | 2.83 | 1.115 | 16.6 |
| Realise firm portfolio diversification operations | 13 | 2.77 | 0.927 | 15.4 |
| Enhance local research and development capacities | 12 | 2.58 | 1.165 | 25.0 |
| Restrict local market competition | 14 | 2.57 | 1.158 | 14.2 |
| Share knowledge and firm management experiences of the acquired firm | 15 | 2.33 | 0.900 | 0.0 |
| Employ management personnel of the acquired firm | 13 | 2.31 | 0.630 | 0.0 |
| Facilitate financing | 12 | 2.08 | 0.900 | 0.0 |

Note: Each measured on a 5-point scale: 1 = very unimportant; 5 = very important.

| Table 6.15 | Motives for strategic alliances |

|  | Sample size | Mean | Standard deviation | % reporting 4 or 5, on a 5-point scale |
|---|---|---|---|---|
| Reduce procurement costs | 80 | 3.96 | 0.770 | 75.1 |
| Enhance local productivity | 70 | 3.73 | 0.883 | 54.3 |
| Share local branding resources | 67 | 3.61 | 1.029 | 52.3 |
| Share local marketing channels | 74 | 3.61 | 0.977 | 50.0 |
| Share knowledge/ technical know-how | 70 | 3.39 | 1.040 | 40.0 |
| Engage in joint efforts in R&D | 67 | 3.37 | 0.998 | 41.8 |
| Spread risks | 66 | 3.26 | 0.882 | 33.3 |

Note: Each measured on a 5-point scale: 1 = very unimportant; 5 = very important.

In the era of global competition, reliance on firms' own resources and capability is not sufficient to overcome all competitive challenges. Strategic alliances help MNC subsidiaries in China to enhance their market position with the help of coalition partners' resources and services to increase the value of the company and to increase shareholders' value. However, at the current stage, MNC subsidiaries in China have not given their priority to strategic alliances in spreading business risks, engaging in R&D and intellectual contributions. MNC subsidiaries in China strategic alliances are still at an early stage in their life cycle, focusing mainly on product and market expansion strategic alliances. Their major strategic assets and resources have been employed for product and market development and for establishing a corporate image. In the early years, domestic Chinese firms lacked core competencies and resources to form complementary strategic partners with MNC subsidiaries. They rely primarily on their parent company network for key knowledge. The future trend will shift to knowledge-based alliances, risk diversification alliances and R&D alliances in their development stage.

## Hypothesis 4: financing strategy

### Context

Parent funding is the most significant funding channel, with two-thirds of respondents identifying it as significant and a mean of more than 3.50 (Table 6.16). MNCs as foreign investors have difficulty securing indirect funding (loans) from the local government and local banks. Funding from the parent company is more accessible for MNC subsidiaries.

### Test of hypotheses

**Hypothesis 4.1: funding channels for MNC subsidiaries in China are significantly different, depending on if they are wholly versus majority foreign-owned.**
ANOVA analysis showed significant differences in the funding channels, depending on if the MNC subsidiaries are wholly versus majority foreign-owned (Table 6.17).

**Table 6.16**  Avenues for financing, statistics

|  | Sample size | Mean | Standard deviation | % reporting 4 or 5 |
|---|---|---|---|---|
| Parent funding | 96 | 3.98 | 1.026 | 67.7 |
| Local direct fundraising | 58 | 3.69 | 1.173 | 58.6 |
| Overseas direct fundraising | 48 | 3.50 | 0.989 | 50.0 |
| Overseas indirect fundraising | 39 | 3.26 | 1.141 | 33.3 |
| China funding | 45 | 3.09 | 1.184 | 28.9 |
| Local indirect fundraising | 37 | 2.92 | 1.064 | 27.0 |

**Table 6.17** Avenues for financing by ownership status, ANOVA

| Financing channels | | Variation | Degree of freedom | Mean variation | F value | Homogeneity of variance | Significance |
|---|---|---|---|---|---|---|---|
| Parent funding | Group | 1.062 | 2 | 0.531 | 0.499 | 0.254 | 0.609 |
| | In group | 98.896 | 93 | 1.063 | | | |
| | Total | 99.958 | 95 | | | | |
| China funding | Group | 12.144 | 2 | 6.072 | 5.152 | 0.872 | ** 0.010 |
| | In group | 49.500 | 42 | 1.179 | | | |
| | Total | 61.644 | 44 | | | | |
| Local direct fundraising | Group | 0.381 | 2 | 0.190 | 0.134 | 2.779 | 0.875 |
| | In group | 78.033 | 55 | 1.419 | | | |
| | Total | 78.414 | 57 | | | | |
| Local indirect fundraising | Group | 0.897 | 2 | 0.448 | 0.382 | 1.014 | 0.685 |
| | In group | 39.860 | 34 | 1.172 | | | |
| | Total | 40.757 | 36 | | | | |
| Overseas direct fundraising | Group | 2.089 | 2 | 1.044 | 1.070 | 0.379 | 0.352 |
| | In group | 43.911 | 45 | 0.976 | | | |
| | Total | 46.000 | 47 | | | | |
| Overseas indirect fundraising | Group | 6.608 | 2 | 3.304 | 2.777 | 0.371 | 0.076 |
| | In group | 42.828 | 36 | 1.190 | | | |
| | Total | 49.436 | 38 | | | | |

Note: ** statistically significant at $\alpha = 0.05$.

The majority of foreign-owned MNC subsidiaries (including joint ventures) report China and other local funding sources to be more significant than do the wholly owned subsidiaries. Compared to the wholly-owned foreign enterprises, the majority foreign-owned MNC subsidiaries have more limited access to the funds from the parent company, but can rely on the Chinese partners to access the Chinese capital resources (Table 6.18).

**Hypothesis 4.2: funding channels for MNC subsidiaries in China are significantly different, depending on the country origin of their parent company.**
Parent funding and local direct fundraising channels vary significantly across MNC subsidiaries with different national origins (Table 6.19).

US MNC subsidiaries report least difference in significance for the different sources of funding, while Japanese and Korean MNC subsidiaries report greatest difference in significance and are most likely to use parent funding or overseas and local direct fundraising (Table 6.20).

**Hypothesis 4.3: funding channels for MNC subsidiaries in China are significantly different, depending on their age.**
MNC subsidiaries in China with different development tenure or age (less than seven years or more than seven years) show differences in financing from the parent company, fund injection and local direct fundraising, while there were no significant differences in other financing avenues (Table 6.21).

The younger MNC subsidiaries rate parent funding as well as local direct fundraising to be more important than do the older MNC subsidiaries (Table 6.22).

**Table 6.18**  Avenues for financing by ownership status, statistics

| | Financing channels | | | | | |
|---|---|---|---|---|---|---|
| | Parent funding | China funding | Local direct fundraising | Local indirect fundraising | Overseas direct fundraising | Overseas indirect fundraising | Number of subsidiaries |
| Wholly foreign-owned | 3.94 | 2.67 | 3.64 | 2.84 | 3.54 | 3.38 | 91 |
| Majority foreign-owned | 4.12 | 3.75 | 3.76 | 3.00 | 3.56 | 3.25 | 34 |

**Table 6.19**  Avenues for financing by country, Kruskal-Wallis

| Financing channels | Chi square stat. value | df | p-value |
|---|---|---|---|
| Parent funding | 7.338 | 3 | 0.06 * |
| China funding | 4.497 | 3 | 0.21 |
| Local direct fundraising | 9.620 | 3 | 0.02 ** |
| Local indirect fundraising | 2.639 | 3 | 0.45 |
| Foreign direct fundraising | 3.298 | 3 | 0.35 |
| Foreign indirect fundraising | 1.687 | 3 | 0.64 |

Note: **significant at $\alpha = 0.05$; *significant at $\alpha = 0.1$.

**Table 6.20**    Avenues for financing by country, statistics

| Country origin | Financing channels | | | | | | | Number of subsidiaries |
|---|---|---|---|---|---|---|---|---|
| | Parent funding | China funding | Local direct fundraising | Local indirect fundraising | Overseas direct fundraising | Overseas indirect fundraising | | |
| US | 3.63 | 2.69 | 3.14 | 2.56 | 3.33 | 3.50 | | 28 |
| Japan | 4.42 | 2.60 | 3.60 | 2.33 | 4.00 | 3.17 | | 22 |
| EU | 4.05 | 3.50 | 3.17 | 3.00 | 3.86 | 3.67 | | 25 |
| Korea | 4.16 | 3.50 | 4.25 | 3.11 | 3.45 | 3.10 | | 43 |

**Table 6.21**    Avenues for financing by age, test

| Financing channels | Mann-Whitney U | Wilcoxon W | Z | p-value |
|---|---|---|---|---|
| Parent fund injection | 677.5 | 2108.5 | -3.136 | 0.002** |
| China fund injection | 198.5 | 408.5 | -0.576 | 0.564 |
| Local direct fundraising | 210 | 645 | -2.922 | 0.003** |
| Local indirect fundraising | 150.5 | 340.5 | -0.052 | 0.959 |
| Foreign direct fundraising | 233 | 611 | -0.55 | 0.583 |
| Foreign indirect fundraising | 130 | 266 | -1.236 | 0.217 |

Note: **statistically significant at $\alpha = 0.05$ level.

**Table 6.22** Avenues for financing by age, statistics

| Firm age (years) | Financing channels | | | | | | |
|---|---|---|---|---|---|---|---|
| | Parent funding | China funding | Local direct fundraising | Local indirect fundraising | Foreign direct fundraising | Foreign indirect fundraising | Number of subsidiaries |
| ≤7 | 4.37 | 3.00 | 4.15 | 2.94 | 3.53 | 2.94 | 52 |
| >7 | 3.68 | 3.27 | 3.34 | 3.00 | 3.41 | 3.38 | 72 |

## *Hypothesis 5: marketing strategy*

### Sales context

Table 6.23 shows that MNC subsidiaries in China generate 47.4 per cent of revenues in China's domestic market, and 52.6 per cent in markets outside of China. This indicates how the subsidiaries have become the MNCs' global manufacturing bases, and how the Chinese domestic market has also become important. The results are consistent with the findings in Chapter 4 that the main motive of MNC investment in China was to open up the Chinese market and establish a production base (Zhao, 2002). For additional investments in later stages, their motives shifted to greater profits and expansion in China.

In the late 1980s and early 1990s, most MNCs were attracted by cheap labour and low-cost resources, with a goal of establishing a Chinese production base. MNC subsidiaries in China started to see a steady increase of internal trade with their parent companies and other subsidiaries in the MNC network. China became the production manufacturing base for the global supply chain of MNCs (Xiao, 2003). In 2003, China's imports and exports attributable to foreign-owned enterprises were $472.2 billion, or 54.8 per cent of China's imports and 56.2 per cent of China's exports. Since then, as the examples

| Table 6.23 | Composition of sales channels, statistics |

|  | N | Mean | Standard deviation |
|---|---|---|---|
| Ratio of products sold within China | 89 | 47.4% | 40.0% |
| Ratio of products sold to the parent firm country | 89 | 28.4% | 34.9% |
| Ratio of products exported to other countries | 89 | 24.2% | 34.1% |

| Table 6.24 | Strategic motives in China of selected MNCs |

| MNC | Strategic goals and motives |
|---|---|
| Siemens | Market leader in the key industries of electrical engineering and electronics industry in China, targeting East Asia |
| Volkswagen | Early mover and market leader in China's auto market, targeting East and Southeast Asian markets to beat Japan and South Korean automobile manufacturers |

in Table 6.24 show, MNC subsidiaries are focusing on becoming a market leader in China and East Asia.

## Local decision-making autonomy

Since the 1960s, there has been controversy on localisation and integration in international marketing research and application. Levitt (1983) believed that the new techniques of communication and transportation and the development of media technologies created an increasing homogenisation of the world market. Therefore, MNCs should focus all their attention on meeting global demand and achieving economies of scale. All the overseas subsidiaries should adopt integrated globalisation marketing strategies. Douglas and Wind (1987) noted that using only integration was too simplistic and not an optimal solution. Prahalad and Doz (1987) proposed an integration–localisation framework and specified that the integration that MNCs confronted came from the pressure of MNC global strategy coordination, while the pressures of localisation came from differences of consumer demand, differences in the distribution channel, the requirements for substitutes and product improvement, market structure and government control.

As noted earlier, a majority of the executives (58.4 per cent) agreed that their firms have a localised marketing policy for firm operations. The immature Chinese market has presented some special features that are different from the relatively stable situation of the Western markets.[1] The Chinese market varies significantly in its national psychology, value orientation, lifestyle and emotional awareness, which all shape special consumer demand and consumption trends. This reality requires MNC subsidiaries in China to draft and implement appropriate strategies according to the peculiarities of the Chinese market.

On all items of local decision-making autonomy in marketing, the ratings of autonomy (1 = very low, 5 = very high) exceeded the midpoint of 3.0, indicating freedom in marketing decision-making. The autonomy was perceived to be greatest in service guarantee, market research and forecasting, distribution channels control, and choice of target market, with means of more than 3.50 (Table 6.25). They had less freedom in key activities that influence the company's long-term development or corporate image. Multinational companies delegated more autonomy to their

| Table 6.25 | Marketing local decision-making autonomy areas, statistics |

| Marketing local decision-making items | N | Mean | Standard deviation |
|---|---|---|---|
| Service guarantee | 88 | 3.73 | 1.014 |
| Market research and forecasting | 98 | 3.60 | 1.173 |
| Distribution channels control and management | 85 | 3.60 | 1.071 |
| Choice of target market | 95 | 3.59 | 1.087 |
| Product pricing | 97 | 3.53 | 1.032 |
| Sales and business promotion | 90 | 3.47 | 1.144 |
| Public relations and public welfare | 84 | 3.44 | 1.034 |
| Advertising | 90 | 3.42 | 1.070 |
| Brand management | 84 | 3.39 | 0.982 |
| Choice of product portfolio | 93 | 3.33 | 1.067 |

Note: 1 = very low autonomy; 5 = very high autonomy.

subsidiaries in China for daily marketing operations, but gave them less authority for strategic decisions.

The correlation between marketing strategy autonomy and marketing localisation was 0.27 ($p < 0.01$, N = 95). Thus, higher autonomy in marketing strategy is correlated positively with greater marketing localisation.

## Key marketing endeavours

Executives were asked to evaluate the importance (1 = very unimportant; 5 = very important) of marketing endeavours in enhancing their marketing capacities (Table 6.26). Customer satisfaction, firm image, customer relationship management and service guarantee were rated as the most important, with means of more than 4.0 on each. Advertising was rated as the least important.

**Table 6.26**    Marketing endeavour areas, statistics

| Marketing endeavours | N | Mean | Standard deviation |
|---|---|---|---|
| Customer satisfaction | 102 | 4.18 | 0.948 |
| Firm image | 96 | 4.03 | 0.956 |
| Customer relationship management | 103 | 4.03 | 0.944 |
| Service guarantee | 95 | 4.01 | 1.016 |
| Brand | 100 | 3.93 | 1.130 |
| Product development and manufacture | 99 | 3.88 | 0.982 |
| Market research and forecasting | 85 | 3.87 | 1.067 |
| Product pricing | 96 | 3.84 | 0.850 |
| Choice of product portfolio | 92 | 3.78 | 0.849 |
| Distribution channels control and management | 87 | 3.71 | 1.066 |
| Marketing and business promotion | 90 | 3.71 | 1.019 |
| Public relations and public welfare | 87 | 3.63 | 1.069 |
| Advertising | 92 | 3.46 | 1.063 |

MNC subsidiaries in China have high awareness of the need and procedures to enhance customer satisfaction, improve corporate image, implement customer relationship management and service assurance so that firms can get closer to their customer and improve the company's image in the marketing strategy. This customer service orientation provided a much greater competitive edge and was very much favoured over the rigid approach to product manufacturing and sales used by the state-owned enterprises. Implementation of customer service-oriented marketing strategy helped MNC subsidiaries in China to redesign marketing strategies and cut down costs according to the service characteristics while ensuring service quality remains the same or is improved. MNC subsidiaries in China showed good examples of how to shift from product-centred firms to service-centred enterprises. The motive was to enhance the overall firm image rather than simply focusing on the branding image of the individual product.

We further investigated marketing endeavours across MNC subsidiaries from different country origins. Due to differences in social and cultural characteristics, and firm values and objectives, the priorities of marketing initiatives and activities vary. For example, American culture is rationalistic, focusing on doing the right things. In decision-making, US executives pay more attention to procedures and efficiency, and are more process-oriented and systematic. For this reason, when they develop marketing strategies, they emphasise the scientific, systematic and standardised aspects. Japanese culture has a strong sense of belonging to society and thus Japanese enterprises have pursued dual objectives in economic efficiency and in serving their country. Their marketing value orientation is often not profit maximisation, but to promote long-term development. In developing a marketing strategy, they put more emphasis on factors such

**Table 6.27** Top three marketing endeavour areas by country

| Rank | US | Japan | EU | South Korea |
|------|-----|-------|-----|-------------|
| 1 | Market research and forecasts | Customer satisfaction | Branding | Customer satisfaction |
| 2 | Customer satisfaction | Service assurance | Customer satisfaction | Customer relation management |
| 3 | Service assurance | Company image | Service assurance | Company image |

as corporate image that influence corporate long-term development (Zhao, 1999b). Consistent with this, Table 6.27 shows that the US MNC subsidiaries pay more attention to market research and forecasting; EU subsidiaries care more about product branding; Japanese and South Korean subsidiaries are more concerned about their corporate image.

## Test of hypotheses

**Hypothesis 5.1: there are significant differences in the export sales ratio of MNC subsidiaries in China with different country origins.**

The export–sales ratio was significantly related with the country of the parent company (chi square = 16.901, df = 3, $p < 0.001$).

As Table 6.28 shows, US MNC subsidiaries have much higher local sales, accounting for three-quarters of their total sales. Japanese MNC subsidiaries are most dependent on sales to parent firm countries, with their sales in Japan being slightly greater than their sales in China. Korean MNC subsidiaries are more focused on sales to third countries.

The investment of US MNCs was primarily for developing the Chinese market and sales in China were the focus of their strategic move. EU multinational companies came to China

| Table 6.28 | Export and domestic sales by country |

| | Domestic sales (%) | Products to parent firm country (%) | Export to other countries (%) |
|---|---|---|---|
| US | 75.56 | 16.67 | 7.78 |
| Japan | 41.27 | 44.12 | 14.79 |
| EU | 53.40 | 34.87 | 10.53 |
| South Korea | 28.69 | 26.03 | 45.28 |

with a similar timeline as those from the United States, but with much less internationalisation. Japan and South Korea had different situational needs. In addition to the Asian economic crisis in 1997 and low production costs in China, domestic industrial policy and persistent high domestic labour costs forced many of their firms to move a large part of the cost centres (manufacturing centres) to China. Their MNC subsidiaries in China not only shouldered the burden of occupying the Chinese market, but also fulfilled tasks of supplying products for the MNC global sales – either directly, as in the case of South Korea, or after further processing in the parent country, as in the case of Japan. Lower transportation costs to Japan further supported this strategy. Therefore, MNC subsidiaries from these two countries had much higher export levels.

**Hypothesis 5.2: there are significant differences in marketing decision-making autonomy, depending on the export sales ratio of MNC subsidiaries in China.**
MNC subsidiaries in China were divided into two groups depending on their export sales ratio (<50 per cent and ≥50 per cent). On three of the variables, the firms with lower export sales ratio had significantly greater marketing decision-making autonomy – market research and forecasting, choice of target markets and advertising (Table 6.29).

| Table 6.29 | Selected marketing decision-making autonomy areas by export ratio, mean differences |
|------------|----------|

|  | Means | | Significance |
|---|---|---|---|
|  | Export-sales ratio ≥50% | Export-sales ratio <50% | P value |
| Market research and forecasting | 3.34 | 3.95 | 0.021 |
| Choice of target markets | 3.37 | 3.92 | 0.030 |
| Advertising | 3.20 | 3.75 | 0.017 |

Because MNC subsidiaries have to adapt their sales moves for products sold in China to satisfy the special needs of users and react to the competitive environment, they need sufficient autonomy to decide how to proceed with market research and forecasting, how to choose the target market and how to advertise and use other resources. In terms of export, because subsidiaries in China play the role of production base, there is no need for a lot of marketing decision-making freedom.

## Hypothesis 6: knowledge transfer strategy

### Context

MNC subsidiaries in China communicate with the parent company mainly through explicit knowledge transfer. Training, information technology and formal conferences were identified as the most important avenues for transmission of knowledge with mean scores of more than 3.50. In contrast, the implicit knowledge transmission avenues of informal personal links, job rotation and cross-functional teams had mean scores of less than 3.50 (Table 6.30).

The KSFs that have the most impact on the knowledge transfer from the parent company to MNC subsidiaries in

| | **Table 6.30** | Areas of knowledge flow with parent, statistics | | |

| | N | Mean | Standard deviation |
|---|---|---|---|
| Training | 105 | 3.97 | 0.882 |
| Information technology | 101 | 3.94 | 0.925 |
| Formal conference | 95 | 3.61 | 0.971 |
| Cross-functional team | 87 | 3.25 | 1.143 |
| Work rotation | 91 | 3.24 | 1.036 |
| Informal personal contacts | 87 | 3.06 | 1.082 |

Note: 1 = very unimportant; 5 = very important.

China are: knowledge resources of the parent company, knowledge and ability of the expatriates from the parent company and training measures. Employee job rotation, implicit knowledge transfer from the parent company and cultural differences – between the parent MNC and the subsidiary organisations, and between the parent MNC country and China – were identified as having least impact (see Table 6.31).

## Test of hypothesis

**Hypothesis 6.1: the avenues for knowledge flow from the parent MNC to the subsidiaries in China vary depending on their industry of operation.**

We ran a test of mean differences on four major sectors of chemical/pharmaceutical, iron and steel/machinery/ engineering, electronic/electrical equipment and light/textile industries (Table 6.32). Only two sectors – iron and steel/ machinery/engineering and light/textile – had significantly different scores for the knowledge flow avenues. MNC subsidiaries in the iron and steel/machinery/engineering sector rate all the avenues significantly higher, while those in the light/textile sector rate all the avenues significantly lower.

| Table 6.31 | KSF impacting knowledge flow with parent, statistics |

| Key success factors | N | Mean | Standard deviation |
|---|---|---|---|
| Knowledge resources of the parent company | 96 | 3.96 | 0.832 |
| Knowledge and ability of expatriates from the parent company | 102 | 3.94 | 0.768 |
| Training measures | 97 | 3.75 | 0.925 |
| Company employees' willingness to learn | 91 | 3.70 | 0.850 |
| Firm position in MNC global network | 93 | 3.61 | 0.978 |
| Company incentive for employee behaviour to accept new knowledge | 90 | 3.61 | 1.035 |
| MNC culture of global knowledge-sharing | 88 | 3.56 | 1.049 |
| Competition intensity in subsidiary's industry | 90 | 3.48 | 1.030 |
| MNC internal network | 88 | 3.44 | 0.981 |
| China's protection measures for intellectual property rights | 87 | 3.40 | 1.028 |
| Cultural differences between China and the home country | 92 | 3.23 | 0.915 |
| Degree of implicit knowledge transfer from the parent company | 84 | 3.21 | 0.919 |
| Culture differences between the parent company and the subsidiary | 88 | 3.19 | 0.882 |
| Employee job rotation between the subsidiary and the parent company | 87 | 3.02 | 1.011 |

Note: 1 = no impact; 5 = significant impact.

The iron and steel/machinery/engineering sector is more technology-intensive, so the attention to knowledge flow from the parent to the subsidiaries is much greater. Conversely, the technology-intensity in the light/textile sector is low, and so is the demand for knowledge flow.

| Table 6.32 | Areas of knowledge flow with parent by industry |

|  | Sectors | | Variance test | | Significant | |
|---|---|---|---|---|---|---|
|  | Iron & steel/ machinery/ engineering | Light/ textile | p-value | t value | df | p-value |
| Information technology | 4.25 | 3.74 | 0.36 | 2.01 | 29 | 0.05 |
| Formal conference | 4.00 | 3.16 | 0.34 | 2.39 | 29 | 0.02 |
| Training | 4.23 | 3.58 | 0.06 | 2.07 | 30 | 0.04 |
| Informal personal contacts | 4.00 | 2.84 | 0.23 | 3.14 | 28 | 0.004 |
|  | 4.00 | 3.09 | 0.93 | 2.18 | 32 | 0.04 |
| Cross-functional team | 3.91 | 2.95 | 0.915 | 2.55 | 28 | 0.02 |

Note: 1 = no impact; 5 = significant impact.

# Hypothesis 7: human resources strategy

## HR decision-making autonomy

International HR strategy is an integral part of multinational companies' global strategy. Because of their unified strategy, technical security and management performance requirements, MNCs usually send technical and management executives to their subsidiaries for HR integration strategy. However, we find a high level of HR localisation to deal with the high expatriation cost and rising nationalism in China. MNC subsidiaries have high control of their human resources functions such as staff recruitment, staff training, and job allocation and performance evaluation. They have trained and prepared a lot of high-quality managerial talents for efficient local management duties.

Executives were asked to rate the area of responsibility in four HR areas (1 = subsidiary fully responsible; 5 = parent

| Table 6.33 | | Areas of HR autonomy, statistics | |
|---|---|---|---|

| | N | Mean | Standard deviation |
|---|---|---|---|
| Performance assessment | 105 | 2.50 | 1.241 |
| Position collocation | 102 | 2.39 | 1.187 |
| Staff training | 108 | 2.37 | 1.235 |
| Staff recruitment | 104 | 2.03 | 1.119 |

fully responsible). The mean scores in each area were less than the midpoint of 3.0, indicating that subsidiaries in China have more responsibility or higher autonomy in decision-making for human resource issues (Table 6.33).

An HR decision-making autonomy was constructed by aggregating the four items in Table 6.33 (reverse-scored). This autonomy measure had a significant negative correlation ($r = -0.24$, $p < 0.05$) with the perceived degree of labour confrontation (1 = very small; 5 = very high) faced by MNC subsidiaries in China. If the subsidiaries can make timely adjustments and change issues in human resource management or other labour-related problems, labour confrontation intensity is relatively low. MNC subsidiaries with more freedom can change improper regulation and rules before negative results occur. They could also make quick changes to adapt to local competitors' moves such as better HR measures and improvement of incentive policies to overcome any sense of inequity for consistent employee working efficiency and commitment. They also find it easier to cultivate psychological recognition in their employees. Once the employees recognise and accept their firms, they have higher efficiency and loyalty, which prevent labour conflicts. In contrast, MNC subsidiaries with weak autonomy have to report labour conflicts and wait for instructions. The whole process has far too many layers of command, thereby contributing to more complicated labour–management conflicts.

## Appointment of key personnel

Table 6.34 shows that more than 90 per cent of both the surveyed chairmen and general managers had been appointed by the parent company. Nearly half of the personnel in these two positions were from the HQ country. In contrast, nearly half of the personnel in the vice general manager and the department manager positions were recruited from mainland China.

The huge market potential in China offers leverage to MNC subsidiaries in supporting the whole MNC network in global deployment. However, many scandals and crises in MNC subsidiaries have made MNCs cognisant of the need to strengthen control of their subsidiaries in China. Thus, MNC headquarters control the key positions and the power of appointment and removal for board chairman and CEO for the subsidiaries in China. Further, MNC parent companies usually appoint or employ top-level executives

**Table 6.34**   Origins of senior leadership, statistics

| Position | Source | N | Percentage |
|---|---|---|---|
| Board chairman | Chinese mainland | 25 | 35.21% |
| | Mother country | 34 | 47.89% |
| | Third country | 12 | 16.90% |
| General manager | Chinese mainland | 25 | 30.49% |
| | Mother country | 42 | 51.22% |
| | Third country | 15 | 18.29% |
| Vice general manager | Chinese mainland | 49 | 47.12% |
| | Mother country | 35 | 33.65% |
| | Third country | 20 | 19.23% |
| Department manager | Chinese mainland | 60 | 50.85% |
| | Mother country | 37 | 31.36% |
| | Third country | 21 | 17.80% |

from those who they know and trust from the native country, and who can communicate well with the parent companies. Top executives from the native country share the same cultural values with the parent company and can get easy acceptance from officials of the parent company for support. They also understand the parent company's strategic intentions. However, given the high costs of expatriates, and since many local executives have gained experience in middle-level positions, MNCs are also open to select non-home senior managers for top management teams.

Nearly half of the personnel in the senior management positions such as vice general manager and the department heads were recruited from the parent country or third other countries.

The surveyed MNC subsidiaries reported to have a total of 396 expatriate department heads. The largest percentage distribution of expatriates was in the accounting, manufacturing and R&D functions (Table 6.35).

## Test of hypotheses

**Hypothesis 7.1: the autonomy in human resource management function varies across MNC subsidiaries in China depending on their country of origin.**

MNCs from different countries are subject to impact of different cultural values and their macro and micro environment factors. We ran a test on four HR practices, taking country origin as grouping variables, to see if there are significant differences in human resource practices for MNC subsidiaries in China from different country origins (Table 6.36).

There was no perceptible difference among subsidiaries of different country origin of their parent company. We found three reasons: (1) Social and cultural factors of the host

**Table 6.35**    Percentage of expatriate department heads by function

| Department | N | percentage |
|---|---|---|
| Accounting | 62 | 15.7% |
| Manufacture | 50 | 12.6% |
| R&D | 48 | 12.1% |
| Strategic planning | 37 | 9.3% |
| Marketing | 34 | 8.6% |
| Sales | 34 | 8.6% |
| HR | 32 | 8.1% |
| Procurement | 29 | 7.3% |
| Administration | 26 | 6.6% |
| Information | 14 | 3.5% |
| Public relations | 9 | 2.3% |
| Service | 9 | 2.3% |
| Logistics | 8 | 2.0% |
| Others | 4 | 1.0% |
| Total | | 100% |

country have a strong impact on HR management in MNC subsidiaries. To inspire enthusiasm in employees and to improve working efficiency, adjustment of policy and procedures are often needed according to the dominant values of local people. This requires all MNCs in China to

**Table 6.36**    HR decision-making autonomy by country, Kruskal-Wallis test

| | Staff recruitment | Staff training | Position collocation | Performance assessment |
|---|---|---|---|---|
| Chi square | 4.620 | 3.064 | 6.812 | 2.033 |
| Freedom | 3 | 3 | 3 | 3 |
| Significant coefficient | 0.202 | 0.382 | 0.078 | 0.566 |

Note: With $\alpha = 0.05$.

have flexibility in making their HR rules according to the local staff characteristics and cultural orientation. (2) MNC parent companies provide principles and guidelines to their overseas subsidiaries in MNC manuals in the area of human resources management and allow flexibility and freedom for their subsidiaries in China to decide on specific actions and measures for implementation. (3) MNCs have increasingly paid more attention to human resources management in interactions and take corresponding measures to integrate different cultural orientations to reduce cultural conflicts.

Since the MNC subsidiaries in China operate in the same host country environment, they share the same management perspectives for running successful firms. These three reasons explain well why there are no significant differences in human resource practices for MNC subsidiaries in China from different country origins.

**Hypothesis 7.2: the degree of labour confrontation faced by MNC subsidiaries in China varies significantly depending on their perceived SWOT.**

Based on the perception of SWOT of the respondents, we conducted a cluster analysis to identify three types of strategic postures for MNC subsidiaries in China: strength–threat cluster, strength–opportunity cluster and weakness–opportunity cluster. The degree of labour confrontation differed significantly across these clusters (chi square = 6.62, df = 2, $p < 0.05$). Table 6.37 and Figure 6.2 show that the subsidiaries that were perceived to have internal strengths but external threats faced the least labour confrontation, while those who were perceived to have internal weaknesses but external opportunities faced the greatest labour confrontation.

From the internal environment perspective, labour confrontation intensity is related to the strengths and capabilities of MNC subsidiaries in China. On the one hand,

| Table 6.37 | Labour confrontation by perceived SWOT postures, statistics | | |
|---|---|---|---|

| SWOT-based clusters | Mean for labour intensity | N | Standard deviation |
|---|---|---|---|
| strength–threat | 1.90 | 21 | 0.889 |
| strength–opportunity | 2.45 | 49 | 1.156 |
| weakness–opportunity | 2.95 | 19 | 1.393 |
| Total | 2.43 | 89 | 1.196 |

Note: 1 = very small; 5 = very high.

with less labour confrontation, the leaders and the followers can unite in pursuit of their missions and vision. Employees have better recognition and buy-in with their enterprises psychologically, which results in high efficiency and productivity. All of this gives rise to competitive advantage in the marketplace. On the other hand, if the company has an advantageous competitive position, employees have better psychological stability and sense of pride, which cultivates their loyalty and commitment.

| Figure 6.2 | Labour confrontations by perceived SWOT postures |
|---|---|

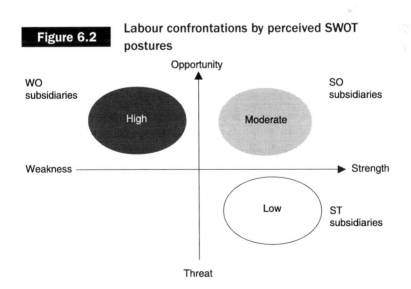

**177**

From the external environment perspective, labour confrontation often represents a firm's lack or delay of responses and actions to satisfy employees' expectations. Under greater market opportunity (SO), employees have higher psychological expectations. If such expectations are not met or are delayed, the labour relations can become vulnerable. When subsidiaries face threats, employees' expectations are lower and people have a sense of responsibility to work with the management team in confronting the difficulties. That is why subsidiaries in ST situations have fewer labour conflicts.

The subsidiaries with a WO position have the greatest labour confrontation because firms have good external opportunities but no internal capabilities to make the best use of them. In addition, they have fewer resources to meet the employees' expectations.

## Hypothesis 8: R&D strategy

### Types of innovations

Respondents rated the importance (1 = very unimportant; 5 = very important) of various types of innovations for MNC subsidiaries in China for enhancing their competitive advantages. Technology and product innovations were rated as the most important with mean scores of more than 4.20 on each, while structural innovation was rated as the least important with a mean of less than 4.0 (Table 6.38).

With the diversification of customer demand and rapid change in customer tastes in China, MNCs need to offer a variety of products in order to quickly deliver the required choice. To achieve new product innovation, technological innovation is a must. In recent years, MNC subsidiaries in China are beginning to serve as the foothold for MNCs' expansion in China and function as technical innovation transferee, while making contributions to enhancing MNC

| Table 6.38 | Significance of various types of innovations, statistics |
|---|---|

|  | N | Mean | Standard deviation | % reporting 4 or 5, on a 5-point scale |
|---|---|---|---|---|
| Technology innovation | 104 | 4.22 | 0.800 | 83.6 |
| Product innovation | 107 | 4.21 | 0.821 | 83.2 |
| Concept innovation | 95 | 4.14 | 0.895 | 75.8 |
| Market innovation | 104 | 4.10 | 0.819 | 75.0 |
| Management innovation | 101 | 4.09 | 0.722 | 80.2 |
| Structure innovation | 90 | 3.98 | 0.874 | 73.3 |

Note: 1 = unimportant; 5 = very important.

technology capabilities. From 1985 to 2003, eight MNCs – Pfizer, Volkswagen, Nokia, Motorola, IBM, Thomson, Philips and Sony – registered a total of 20,350 patents in China. Since the 1990s, the number of patent applications from MNC subsidiaries in China has been growing annually by around 30 per cent. The growth is particularly strong in emerging areas such as communications, computers and medicine (Mao, 2005).

## Sources of R&D funding

Respondents were asked to rate the importance (1 = very unimportant, 5 = very important) of various sources of R&D funding. A large proportion (48.4 per cent) of the sample executives believed that it is very important that MNC subsidiaries obtain R&D capital with their own efforts, with a mean score of 3.35 (Table 6.39).

## Locus of R&D decision-making

Table 6.40 shows that 31.4 per cent of the R&D projects are decided completely by the MNC subsidiaries in China, while the parent company plays a role of varying importance in the

| Table 6.39 | Significance of various R&D funding sources, statistics |

| R&D funding sources | N | Mean | Standard deviation | % reporting 4 or 5, on a 5-point scale |
|---|---|---|---|---|
| Firms' own funds | 62 | 3.35 | 1.356 | 48.4 |
| Funds from parent company | 53 | 2.34 | 1.440 | 22.6 |
| Funds from Chinese partners | 24 | 1.83 | 1.204 | 16.7 |
| Funds from China's non-governmental organisations and agencies | 21 | 1.57 | 1.076 | 9.5 |
| Funds from home government subsidy | 25 | 1.56 | 0.961 | 8.0 |
| Funds from non-governmental organisations and agencies of the home country | 21 | 1.48 | 0.873 | 0.0 |

Note: 1 = very unimportant; 5 = very important.

other 68.6 per cent of projects. Further analysis suggested that the degree of autonomy in R&D decision-making was positively correlated (Kendall's tau-b = 0.24, $p < 0.01$; N = 46) with R&D investment rate (R&D as a proportion of sales revenues).

| Table 6.40 | Decision modes for R&D projects, statistics |

| | N | % |
|---|---|---|
| R&D projects identified, developed and implemented by subsidiaries | 22 | 31.4 |
| R&D projects identified and assigned to subsidiaries by parent company for their development | 17 | 24.3 |
| R&D projects identified by subsidiaries but some of the major components need approval from the parent company | 20 | 28.6 |
| R&D projects identified by subsidiaries but need approval from the parent company | 11 | 15.7 |

## Procedures to enhance R&D capabilities

Executives were asked to evaluate the importance (1 = very unimportant; 5 = very important) of various procedures to enhance R&D capabilities. The most important procedures were identified as increasing R&D investments, improving R&D personnel quality and setting up specialised R&D institutions, with mean scores of more than 3.50 on each, and more than 50 per cent of the respondents identifying these as important or very important. In contrast, providing funds for internal technological projects was deemed least important (Table 6.41).

## Importance of intellectual property rights

We found that a measure of perceived protection of intellectual property rights in China was positively correlated

| Table 6.41 | Significance of procedures to enhance R&D capabilities, statistics | | | |
|---|---|---|---|---|
| Procedures to enhance R&D capabilities | N | Mean | Standard deviation | % reporting 4 or 5, on a 5-point scale |
| Increase R&D investment and expenditure | 76 | 3.61 | 1.108 | 56.6 |
| Improve R&D personnel quality via recruitment and training | 76 | 3.59 | 1.157 | 63.2 |
| Set up specialised R&D institutions | 81 | 3.53 | 1.141 | 54.3 |
| Cooperate with Chinese universities and scientific research institutions | 73 | 3.22 | 1.336 | 48.0 |
| Cooperate with other companies for technology and research projects | 68 | 3.15 | 1.175 | 41.2 |
| Provide funds for internal technological projects | 67 | 2.73 | 1.136 | 23.9 |

(p < 0.001) with the importance rating on all the procedures to improve the research and development conditions. Therefore, the better the perceived protection of intellectual property in China, the better the environmental conditions to improve research and development capabilities by MNC subsidiaries (Table 6.42).

## Test of hypotheses

**Hypothesis 8.1: the innovation initiatives by MNC subsidiaries in China vary depending on their country of origin.**

MNC subsidiaries from Japan put stronger emphasis on three types of innovations – product, management and market – than do those from the US and South Korea. The degree of emphasis for EU subsidiaries is not significantly different from those of the Japanese subsidiaries (Table 6.43).

**Hypothesis 8.2: the innovation initiatives by MNC subsidiaries in China vary depending on their industry of operation.**

There were no overall significant differences in innovation initiatives across different industries. Only one exception was found in the pair-wise comparisons. Management innovation for the chemical/pharmaceutical sector is perceived to be more significant than in the electronics/ electrical equipment sector (p < 0.05; df = 38). Historically, the chemical/pharma-ceutical sector put greater emphasis on product and technological innovations. In recent years, to meet intensifying competition, there is a growing recognition of the role and significance of management of innovation. On the other hand, the electronic/electrical equipment industry has been in a highly competitive condition for a long time and thus management and structural innovation mechanisms are more mature (Table 6.44).

**Table 6.42** Procedures to enhance R&D capabilities by strength of IPR protection, Kendall's Tau correlation

| | | Procedures to enhance R&D capabilities | | | | | |
|---|---|---|---|---|---|---|---|
| | | Set up specialised R&D institutions | Increase R&D investment and expenditure | Cooperate with Chinese universities and scientific research institutions | Provide funds for internal technological projects | Improve R&D personnel quality via recruitment and training | Cooperate with other companies for technology and research projects |
| **Protection of host intellectual property rights** | Correlation coefficient | 0.309*** | 0.424*** | 0.455*** | 0.387*** | 0.387*** | 0.325*** |
| | Sig. | 0.003 | 0.000 | 0.0001 | 0.0001 | 0.001 | 0.002 |
| | N | 65 | 64 | 62 | 59 | 63 | 62 |

Note: *** statistically significant with α = 0.01 (two-tail test).

**Table 6.43** Selected innovation types by country, mean difference test

| | Country | | | | Variance test | | | Mean significance | |
|---|---|---|---|---|---|---|---|---|---|
| | US | Japan | EU | Korea | p-value | t test | df | | p-value |
| Product innovation | 3.96 | 4.57 | | | 0.348 | -2.830 | 35 | | 0.008 |
| | 3.96 | | 4.37 | | 0.341 | -2.143 | 40 | | 0.038 |
| | | 4.57 | | 4.05 | 0.300 | 1.826 | 53 | | 0.074 |
| Management innovation | 3.84 | 4.39 | | | 0.527 | -2.566 | 41 | | 0.014 |
| Market innovation | | 4.44 | | 3.91 | 0.048 | 2.654 | 46 | | 0.011 |

**Table 6.44** Innovation types by industry, statistics

| Sectors | Product innovation | Market innovation | Technology innovation | Management innovation | Organisation structure innovation | Concept innovation |
|---|---|---|---|---|---|---|
| Chemical/ pharmaceutical | 4.43 | 4.33 | 4.58 | 4.50 | 4.30 | 4.40 |
| Iron and steel/ machinery/ engineering | 4.46 | 4.25 | 4.45 | 4.18 | 3.90 | 4.18 |
| Electronic/electrical equipment | 4.14 | 4.11 | 4.23 | 3.93 | 3.83 | 4.35 |
| Light/textile | 4.14 | 3.95 | 4.29 | 4.24 | 4.24 | 4.05 |

Many scholars have noted that MNCs historically have focused their attention only on ways of establishing R&D centres in China and to core technology transfer from the parent companies. They have overlooked R&D capabilities needed for development and adaptation of MNC subsidiaries in the local market. MNC subsidiaries in China are facing fierce competition from foreign multinationals and local enterprises. China's domestic enterprises have upgraded their R&D capabilities through access to advanced technology and equipment and purchase of patents. This in turn has increased the speed of technology transfer from the parent companies to sustain subsidiaries' competitive position. Although MNC subsidiaries in China rely on the parent company for patent technology transfer to enhance R&D, they also function as MNC explorers and executors in the Chinese market. They are responsible for R&D localisation and transformation of technology for local use and application. Localisation has a positive impact on the development and the success rate in R&D of MNC subsidiaries in China.

## Hypothesis 9: strategy blunders

### Types of strategic blunders

Executives were asked to identify their most significant area of strategic blunder: 21.5 per cent identified the most significant strategic blunder to be in HR management and 16.8 per cent identified it to be in marketing. Lack of good understanding of Chinese local personnel idiosyncrasies and Chinese market consumer demand are thus the major factors impeding appropriate strategic planning and actions by MNC subsidiaries in China (Table 6.45).

| Table 6.45 | Percentage distribution of most significant strategic blunder | | |

| | N | Percentage |
|---|---|---|
| HR management | 23 | 21.5% |
| Marketing | 18 | 16.8% |
| R&D | 11 | 10.3% |
| Product portfolio | 10 | 9.3% |
| Manufacturing | 7 | 6.5% |
| Strategic alliance | 6 | 5.6% |
| Merger and acquisition | 5 | 4.7% |
| Logistics | 3 | 2.8% |
| Others | 3 | 2.8% |
| Finance management | 2 | 1.9% |

## Reasons for strategic blunders

Respondents rated their agreement (1 = strongly disagree; 5 = strongly agree) with the various reasons for their strategic blunders. The top two reasons were: cross-cultural management conflict and lack of resources and support from the parent company, with mean scores of more than 3.25 on each. Global strategy adjustment is another key factor (Table 6.46).

These reasons are explained below.

Each culture has its specific social environment and its own system of values and codes of conduct, which impact people's behaviours, beliefs, habits and social structures. MNCs are often unable to understand the distinctive Chinese culture and promptly adjust management styles and methods, which leads to strategic mistakes.

In a multinational network, subsidiaries can seek support and resources from the parent company and other subsidiaries based on their strategic needs, but the parent company has final decision-making power for the internal allocation of resources. Whether the parent company provides such

| Table 6.46 | Reasons for strategic blunders, statistics |
|---|---|

|  | Mean |
|---|---|
| Chinese and foreign cross-cultural management conflict | 3.38 |
| Lack of resources and support from the parent company | 3.3 |
| Adjustment of the parent company's global strategy | 3.22 |
| Underestimation of competition intensity in host markets | 3.11 |
| Error in judgement for host market capacity and its potential | 3.1 |
| Inefficient management thanks to 'huge firm syndrome' | 3.06 |
| Ineffective management and control over suppliers and vendors | 3 |
| Underestimation of instability of the host environment | 2.98 |
| Difference in strategic goals for joint venture partners | 2.94 |
| Relations with the local government and the public | 2.71 |
| Labour disputes | 2.52 |

Note: 1 = strongly disagree; 5 = strongly agree.

support and how much support will be provided depends on the parent company's global strategy and the bargaining power of the subsidiaries. In the early stages, many MNCs regarded China as a production base and investment in China was mainly concentrated in the assembly of low value-added processing sectors. Most did not provide advanced technology and other resources such as management experiences and skills to their subsidiaries in China. With expansion of the Chinese market and intensification of scale-based competition, the existing resources and inputs became increasingly insufficient for additional growth to satisfy the global strategy adjustment need of the parent company. It has been very difficult for MNC subsidiaries to obtain R&D and technology capabilities and improve their management skills in a short period of time; this has contributed to strategic mistakes.

Finally, when the parent company plans to make global strategic adjustment, it needs its subsidiaries' cooperation. If the subsidiaries continue to seek their own development and strategy implementation, inconsistent with the parent company's strategic global demand, the parent company will interfere with the subsidiaries' strategic decisions. This results in strategic mistakes. Strategic blunders will also occur if the parent company's global strategy adjustment is not in line with the world economic development trend, or if the strategy of subsidiaries in China does not fit in with the Chinese reality. In addition, underestimating Chinese market competition, market capacity, and market potential and instability, bureaucracy and the slow response to the crisis caused by big enterprise disease are other factors contributing to strategic blunders of MNC subsidiaries in China.

## Summary

Table 6.47 summarises various corporate and functional strategies hypotheses.

| Table 6.47 | Hypotheses testing results summary | |
|---|---|---|
| **Hypotheses group** | **Hypotheses** | **Testing result** |
| 1 Relationships with the parent company and with other subsidiaries | 1.1: Strength of ties of MNC subsidiaries in China with the parent company varies significantly depending on the time of their entry in China. | Not substantiated |
| | 1.2: Strength of ties of MNC subsidiaries in China with the MNC network varies significantly depending on the national origin of the parent company. | Substantiated |
| | 1.3: Strength of ties of MNC subsidiaries in China with the parent company varies significantly depending on the location of the headquarters. | Substantiated |
| 2 Integration and localisation | 2.1 Integration and localisation pressures for MNC subsidiaries in China vary depending on their time of entry into China. | Partly substantiated |

| Hypotheses group | Hypotheses | Testing result |
|---|---|---|
| 3 M&A and alliance strategy | No hypothesis was advanced. | |
| 4 Financing strategy | 4.1: Funding channels for MNC subsidiaries in China are significantly different, depending on if they are wholly versus majority foreign-owned. | Substantiated |
| | 4.2: Funding channels for MNC subsidiaries in China are significantly different, depending on the country origin of their parent company. | Substantiated |
| | 4.3: Funding channels for MNC subsidiaries in China are significantly different, depending on their age. | Substantiated |
| 5 Marketing strategy | 5.1: The export–sales ratio of MNC subsidiaries in China varies significantly depending on the national origin of the parent companies. | Substantiated |
| | 5.2: The marketing decision-making autonomy varies significantly depending on the export ratio of MNC subsidiaries in China. | Substantiated |
| 6 Knowledge transfer strategy | 6.1: The avenues for knowledge flow from the parent MNC to the subsidiaries in China vary depending on their industry of operation. | Substantiated |
| 7 Human resources strategy | 7.1: The autonomy in human resource management function varies across MNC subsidiaries in China depending on their country of origin. | Not Substantiated |
| | 7.2: The degree of labour confrontation faced by the MNC subsidiaries in China varies significantly depending on their perceived SWOT. | Substantiated |
| 8 R&D strategy | 8.1: The innovation initiatives by MNC subsidiaries in China vary depending on their country of origin. | Substantiated |
| | 8.2: The innovation initiatives by MNC subsidiaries in China vary depending on their industry of operation. | Not substantiated |
| 9 Strategy blunders | No hypothesis was advanced. | |

# Note

1    Jiaxun He, Hua Zhang (2004). China on international
     marketing and localisation progress of the study. *Beijing
     University Business Journal* (Social Science Edition). 19(2):
     29–33.

# Part 4
# Conclusions

# 7

# Conclusions

**Abstract:** In this chapter, we conclude with a discussion of the stylised growth and development strategy system and behaviour of MNC Chinese subsidiaries, based on the empirical findings.

**Key words:** Growth and development, strategy, MNC overseas subsidiaries, strategic system, implications, practitioners, researchers.

This study focused on the growth and development strategies of MNC subsidiaries in China. We analysed the roles and strategic choices for overseas subsidiaries of multinational corporations. On this basis, we tested hypotheses on the 15 areas of subsidiary operations. Detailed empirical analyses were carried out to discover the reasons and causes for initiatives adopted by MNC subsidiaries in China and their parent companies.

## Growth and development strategies

The growth and development of overseas subsidiaries is influenced and constrained in unique ways by such factors as strategic objective, external environment and resources. There is a need for a systemic analysis of the growth and development modes, and of the issues affecting the growth and development strategies. The strategy in overseas subsidiaries is influenced by both the parent company and the host government. To adapt to the local environment and MNC global business operations, constant strategy adjustments must be made.

The growth and development of the network is realised within the policy framework of the parent company. The parent companies control the overall strategic orientation for growth and development, while providing some degree of strategic autonomy for overseas subsidiaries. This enables a process for growth and development whereby overseas subsidiaries adapt to the environmental changes in the host country. There are two special mechanisms for growth and the development of multinational subsidiaries: (1) the mechanism to determine the initial role of the overseas subsidiaries and the evolution of the strategic role in the MNC network; and (2) selection mechanism for the growth and development strategy of overseas subsidiaries. In their life cycle, overseas subsidiaries play different roles at different stages to accomplish different strategic missions. The choice of strategy for growth and development of overseas subsidiaries should be synchronised with the role of overseas subsidiaries assigned by the parent company for its global network. In the process of growth and development, overseas subsidiaries play a different role and their strategy at different stages changes, with the accumulation of competitive capabilities, changes in value and behaviour of the parent company and changes in the external environment.

The role mechanism and strategy choice mechanism interact with each other to create synergies for growth and development strategy of MNC overseas subsidiaries. This interaction for synergistic effects is a very important part of the theoretical research on the growth and development strategy of multinational subsidiaries. In addition, it is important to consider stages of subsidiaries' life cycle, and the behaviours and performances in different functional areas. Figure 7.1 is

**Figure 7.1**  Research model for growth and development strategy

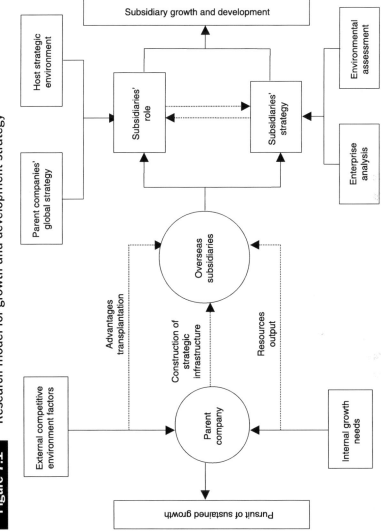

the framework used for this theoretical research for growth and development strategy of MNC subsidiaries.

## Growth and development mechanism

The analysis of mechanisms is the basis of theoretical studies on growth and development of multinational subsidiaries. The mechanisms for the growth and development of multinational subsidiaries are divided into the internal network and the external environment (Figure 7.2).

### Internal network mechanism

The growth and development of overseas subsidiaries within the internal network involves the allocation of resources and a transformation process. Overseas subsidiaries engage in the interactive resource exchanges of output and input with the parent companies and other overseas subsidiaries in the MNC network. In the process of resources-sharing and competition, the role and the strategies of overseas subsidiaries are constantly adjusted and changed.

**Figure 7.2**    Mechanism formulation elements

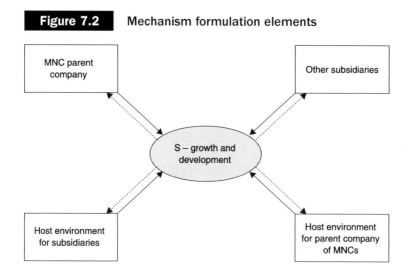

*Resources inflow and outflow mechanism
of the parent company*

MNCs establish an overseas subsidiary to sustain growth of the parent company and to acquire resources to meet growth requirements. In order to improve the efficiency of the resources acquisition and allocation, the parent company exports many resources required for the growth and development of overseas subsidiaries. These resources include tangible and intangible resources. Tangible resources include a firm's infrastructure, funding, equipment, general raw materials and employees. Intangible resources, also known as ownership advantages (Dunning, 1981), include management model of the parent company, brand image, information and product technology. For overseas subsidiaries, the ownership advantages are key resources that determine operational advantages and growth characteristics of overseas subsidiaries.

Overseas subsidiaries use resources from the parent company to build the strategic infrastructure and transform a portion of the host resources to the strategic resources needed by the parent company, which are exported to the parent company. The transformation and output of resources are synergic and supportive of the parent company's global strategic intentions (Prahalad and Doz, 2001).

*Subsidiaries resource-sharing and
competition mechanism*

Overseas subsidiaries are operating in different countries and have three major characteristics in common: (1) they are linked by a common shared ownership; (2) they share resources, such as brands, information, financial resources and credit; (3) as a whole, they implement a common strategy and have the same goal to obtain maximum profits and reduce risks in MNCs.

MNC overseas subsidiaries have independent resources and capacities to form a highly integrated and cooperative network. They can respond flexibly to the local market demand, while they can share the benefits of the integration of manufacturing and usage of network resources. They can access resources required for growth and development inside the parent company network through internal benchmarking (Birkinshaw and Hood, 1998a) and resources-sharing. During the process of their growth and development, they accumulate local advantages and undergo strategy change because of the evolution in their roles in the MNC network. The role change influences the position and status within the network and internal competition for more allocation of resources.

## External environment mechanism

External mechanism refers to the interactive relations between the host and the home country environmental factors that influence the growth of overseas subsidiaries. MNC subsidiaries must adapt to the complex changes in the external environment of the host country. Host government is a major factor influencing MNC overseas subsidiaries and its motives and methods have a critical impact on the growth of overseas subsidiaries.

### Interactions between the host government and overseas subsidiaries

Overseas subsidiaries offer a package of resources to the host government. These include direct resources, such as the multinational ownership of assets, as well as indirect resources, such as the host employment expansion opportunities and thus improvement of living standards of local people. To access these resources, the host government has to provide local resources to MNC overseas subsidiaries, including not only appropriate labour and raw materials but also huge market capacity and potentials. The host government provides policy support and favourable incentive procedures to encourage MNC overseas subsidiaries to operate and develop in the host country. During this interactive process of resources inflow and outflow, the goals of overseas subsidiaries differ from those of the host government. The host government seeks to promote development for the local country, while the MNC overseas subsidiaries try to increase their own competitiveness.

If the host government's objectives are not met, according to the ecological system theory, part of the dissatisfaction in output will be converted to input (Putti and Weihrich, 1999). For instance, the dissatisfaction against overseas subsidiaries from the host government may be converted to the negative interference against MNC subsidiaries. The conflicts caused by interference and resistance have a direct impact on the growth and development of overseas subsidiaries.

### The environmental factors in host countries

The complexity and dynamics of the host operating environment also affects the growth and development of overseas subsidiaries. Several host environments have a larger impact on MNC overseas subsidiaries, including the market environment, the political environment, legal environment, social and cultural environment and geographical environment.

### The MNC home external environment

The home external environment of MNCs has an indirect impact on the development of overseas subsidiaries. They affect the strategic direction of the parent company, which then transfers those by shaping the strategic mission and strategic objectives for overseas subsidiaries. Take the Asian financial crisis as an example. As the South Korean domestic economy suffered from the crisis, South Korean MNCs withdrew their multinational subsidiaries from China.

## MNC subsidiaries' roles

In this study, we analysed different roles that multinational subsidiaries play in the MNC internal network. We found that the roles of Chinese subsidiaries are mixed, with the subsidiaries performing both the initiative role and the strategic role.

### The initial roles of MNC subsidiaries

Because of differences in the host environment, the motives of MNC investment vary. The strategic motives of the parent company determine the strategic direction for overseas subsidiaries in the host country. Building strategic infrastructure and providing strategic resources to the MNC network are the most commonly seen initial roles assigned to the overseas subsidiaries by the parent company. The initial roles of overseas subsidiaries may be divided into six categories:

#### 1 Resource-oriented

The strategic motive for this type of subsidiary is to obtain access to the host country's tangible resources, especially natural resources. In order to accomplish upstream integration and further control of the natural resources needed for growth, MNCs set up overseas subsidiaries in the host country that have the strategic resources they need. The major role of this type of MNC subsidiary is to become engaged in the acquisition of raw materials. The aim is to reduce transaction costs and raw material costs, and help the parent company accumulate strengths and capabilities.

## 2 Production bases

These overseas subsidiaries focus on the use of cheap labour and land resources in the production process to reduce the cost of products. In order to increase production efficiency and lower production cost, MNCs set up overseas subsidiaries in regions or countries with low labour costs. The role of overseas subsidiaries for labour-intensive MNCs is cost oriented.

## 3 Market expansion

When market size and operational scale restrict growth or if there are opportunities for further growth, MNCs seek potential markets with greater capacity.

## 4 Profits focus

The overriding purpose of these subsidiaries is to achieve the maximum profit and serve as a cash cow for the parent company to compensate for the high risk of its global business and international operations. Since there are different views for profit maximisation, profit objectives of MNC subsidiaries may be classified into two categories: (1) the pursuit of high profits; and (2) the pursuit of a satisfactory profit. The excessive profits pursued by MNC subsidiaries might be realised by product pricing strategy and internal price transfer within the MNC network.

## 5 Knowledge extraction

In order to acquire advanced technology and experience in the host country as well as information resources that are extremely beneficial to the growth and development of the parent company, MNCs set up overseas subsidiaries to recruit local talent or directly acquire existing firms to get access to technology, information and knowledge (Fang, 2000). These MNCs are willing to give up a certain amount of profit and market share in exchange for knowledge and information from the host country.

### 6 Risk-diversifying

When threatened by the competition, the parent company may transfer its operations to a country where it has competitive advantages to diversify its business risks, or may directly enter the competitors' market to reduce the competition risk in the domestic market (Vernon, Wells and Rangan, 2000).

## Strategic evolutionary roles of MNC subsidiaries

The accumulated localisation competitive advantages and capabilities of MNC subsidiaries can enhance the strategic position and status of a subsidiary in its MNC network but can also weaken that strategic position. Different competitive advantages and capabilities determine the significance of the subsidiaries in the MNC system and thus their strategic positions vary in the MNC global network. MNC subsidiaries with a stronger position enjoy more strategic autonomy and resource-allocation priority from the parent company.

The strategic evolution of MNC subsidiaries' roles manifests in the changes in their strategic autonomy, global resource allocation priority, reliance on the parent company and nature of the local value chain system for the MNC network. We found that in the process of growth and development, there are three different types of MNC subsidiaries in China.

### 1 Totally subordinated

This type of subsidiary follows the instructions of the parent company and its business arrangements are within the boundaries of the parent company's strategy and policy framework. Most of the Chinese subsidiaries play such a strategic role in the initial stage of entry into China, because at this time they have not yet formed unique competences and competitive advantages. They have relatively limited scope of functions and are highly integrated in the global network.

### 2 Relatively independent

With the continuous accumulation of localisation capacity and the competitive advantages in the growth and development process, these MNC overseas subsidiaries gain increasing strategic autonomy and enjoy relative independence in strategy crafting and implementation. They have penetrated significant local and regional markets, and have secured the freedom to develop new business in new markets. These subsidiaries have the power to demur or modify the assigned tasks or assignment by the parent company in accordance with local needs.

### 3 Central leadership

These subsidiaries have leadership position in a regional or global arena of the MNC and have a high degree of strategic autonomy. They have a great impact on the parent company's global strategy and, therefore, they play a central leadership role in the MNC network. The structural background of MNC overseas subsidiaries is highly globalised integration but highly localised operation.

## Mode and stage of subsidiary role evolution

MNCs change their strategic motives to adapt to environmental changes at home and in the host countries. Such a change can directly lead to adjustment or change in the initial role of MNC overseas subsidiaries. This evolution of role change is no longer passive in nature. MNC subsidiaries accumulate competitive advantages and capabilities in localisation and thus enhance their strategic position in the MNC network.

They actively change their subordinate role and start to play a more significant role in the MNC network.

In our study, we discovered that in their efforts to enhance their strategic position, Chinese subsidiaries have gone through three stages of role evolution: strategic implementation stage, strategic progressive stage and strategic dominance stage (Figure 7.3).

Only in very special circumstances, the overseas subsidiaries' evolution advances by leaps and bounds, for instance, when the parent company needs to shoulder a greater risk for the enhancement of the overseas subsidiary's strategic position. Overseas subsidiaries' strategic position could also decrease or weaken from the parent company's global strategy adjustment and stability (or degeneration). This decline may not follow any law or pattern. Thereby, strategic role evolution of overseas subsidiaries has been portrayed using a snakes and ladders model (Delaney, 1998). Table 7.1 present the features of MNC subsidiaries' strategic role evolution in each stage.

In the growth and development process, MNC subsidiaries become more familiar with the host country's market environment and increase their investment scale. They expand their business areas and market segments and make progress in localisation. This results in the expansion of strategic autonomy and the enhancement of strategic independence; and the integration of all value chain activities from the original single function. They also expand their business scope from basic simple non-core business activities into the MNC's core business areas; and from host country single markets to multi-regional diversified markets. As they set up a local supply chain network, their procurement rate within the internal MNC network is gradually reduced. Their reliance on the parent company's products also reduces, as they become a part of the multinational supply hub for the entire network.

**Figure 7.3** Map of MNC subsidiaries' role evolution

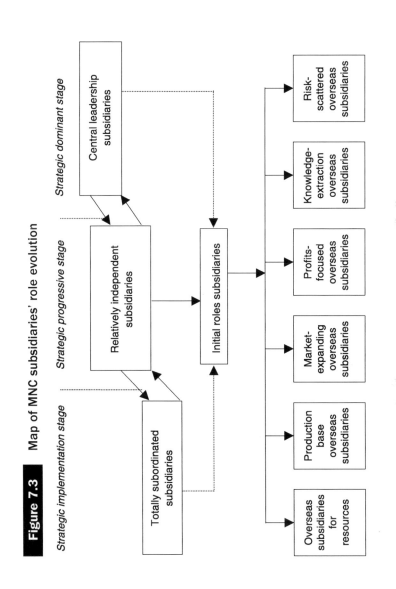

**Table 7.1** Overseas subsidiaries' evolution stages and features

| Evolution stage | Strategic implementation stage | Strategic progressive stage | Strategic dominant stage |
|---|---|---|---|
| Types | Totally subordinated overseas subsidiaries | Independent overseas subsidiaries | Central leadership subsidiaries |
| Strategic target | 1 Implement the strategic intention of the parent company, complete the strategic mission of the parent company.<br>2 Familiarise markets, operation and management in the host country.<br>3 Assess investment risk and reward.<br>4 Develop a long-term partnership image that can help the economic development of the host country in the eyes of the government. | 1 Expand investment and establish regional overseas subsidiaries.<br>2 Train and build local capacities and competitive advantages.<br>3 Formulate growth objectives and intentions.<br>4 Expand market shares. | 1 Build local company network.<br>2 Become regional or global strategic centre.<br>3 Influence the parent company's global strategy.<br>4 Become an important source of profit for the parent company. |
| Operation features | 1 Parent company's non-core and simple industry (labour-intensive industry).<br>2 Centralised management.<br>3 Single market niche. | 1 Capital involved and technology intensive in core industries.<br>2 Gradually diversified operational areas.<br>3 Active expansion in host market and surrounding regional markets. | 1 Control MNC core industries.<br>2 Improve management to control large-scale operations.<br>3 Become the leader in the host country; and become regional or global market centres. |

| Formation of value chain | Engage in functions in a single value chain (production, logistics and marketing). | Integration of high-end and low-end functions and activities, from basic activities to support activities. | Complete value chain system. |
| --- | --- | --- | --- |
| Strategic autonomy | Low | Low | Strong |
| Dependence on the parent company | Strong | Strong | Low |
| Internal procurement rate | High | High | Low |
| Global resources distribution | Low | High | Medium |
| Localised level | Very low | High | Higher |
| Integration level | High | Higher | Highest |

# MNC subsidiaries' strategy choice mechanism

MNC overseas subsidiaries function in the host environment and have to deal with the complex and ever-changing challenges of local and international competitors. To accomplish the strategic mission, they must choose the growth strategy that can adapt to the environment and can make the best use of competitive core competences. The choice of appropriate strategy of overseas subsidiaries is established based on the growth and development mechanism controlled by the parent company and constrained by the host environment factors. All of these factors and their interactions affect strategy choice for overseas subsidiaries and constitute a unique strategic selection mechanism of overseas subsidiaries in their growth and development process.

## S-SWOT analysis for MNC overseas subsidiaries

When crafting growth strategy, MNC overseas subsidiaries need to analyse the internal and external environments and identify firm strengths, weaknesses, market opportunities and threats. The complicated and unique growth and development mechanism makes the MNC overseas subsidiaries' strategy choice different from that of other firms and organisations. We called this unique subsidiary situation analysis the S-SWOT analysis framework for MNC overseas subsidiaries (Figure 7.4).

When MNC overseas subsidiaries conduct structure–environment analysis, they need to consider not only environmental factors of the host country but also those of the home country of the parent company. Their strategy has to be consistent with the role assigned by the MNC and help them survive in the host's general external environment. In conducting internal analysis, MNC subsidiaries not only

**Figure 7.4** S-SWOT analysis framework for MNC subsidiaries

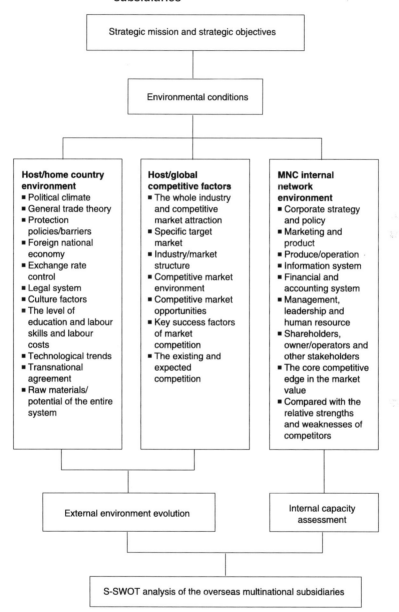

assess their own internal capacities but also consider the core competences in the MNC internal network for the synergistic effects of the multinational cooperation network. The final selection and implementation of the growth and development strategy of overseas subsidiaries is bound and constrained by the subsidiaries' role mechanism and the effect of the parenting advantage of MNCs. Consequently, the S-SWOT analysis for MNC subsidiaries is different from the traditional SWOT analysis for other firms (Figure 7.5).

## Restriction and constraints on role mechanism

The traditional SWOT analysis is based on a firm's complete independence and autonomy in strategy choice, while the S-SWOT analysis for MNC overseas subsidiaries is supported by the reality that most MNC subsidiaries are not fully strategically independent because their role mechanism still restricts the choice of strategy. MNC overseas subsidiaries' strategic selection needs to be subordinate to the parent company's global strategy. The very fact that the MNC parent company can deny the subsidiaries' strategy proposition is the best reflection of role constraint mechanism to bind the subsidiaries' growth and development choice in strategy. On occasions, out of the need for strategic adjustment by the parent company, the interests of overseas subsidiaries are sacrificed for the long-term benefits of the entire MNC system. For these overseas subsidiaries, it is not possible to establish the strategy choice based on traditional strategic thinking.

The choice of the MNC's own growth and development also influence the choice of strategy of MNC overseas subsidiaries. Consider a case where the subsidiary is in an advantageous position in the host country and should adopt the growth strategy. However, the parent company needs to reorganise global operations and consider rebuilding competitive advantage and core capacity for the MNC

**Figure 7.5** Selection framework for overseas subsidiaries' growth and development strategy

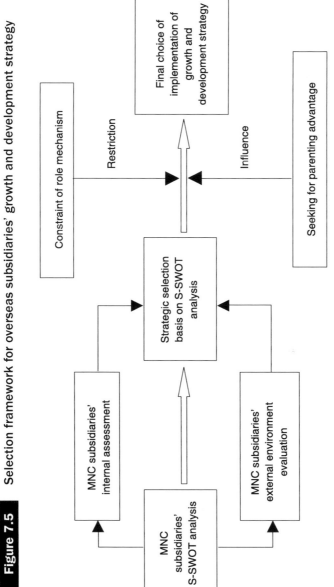

system. The overseas subsidiaries have to adapt to this strategy and may even have to sell or abandon their core business for the sake of the MNC system.

When the strategic position of MNC subsidiaries is lower in the MNC network, the autonomy of these subsidiaries in choosing their own growth and development strategy is smaller. With the enhancement of overseas subsidiaries' strategic position in global competition, the influencing power over the strategy for the entire MNC system is increasing. The choice of overseas subsidiaries' growth and development strategy is focusing more on interactions among firms in the internal system and with firms in the global market.

## Effect of parenting advantage on overseas subsidiaries' growth and development strategic choice

Parenting advantage is the internal network advantage of MNCs. MNC subsidiaries can make good use of this internal network leverage to increase their own competitive capabilities and competitive edge. When the subsidiaries assess internal competences for competitive advantage and disadvantage in the host country, they include the parenting advantage in such a comparison with their competitors. This is one of the unique features of S-SWOT analysis for MNC overseas subsidiaries.

When choosing a growth and development strategy, MNC overseas subsidiaries seek the support of parenting advantage from the parent company and other subsidiaries. However, the parent company owns the final decision-making power for internal resource allocation. Whether to infuse parenting advantage or how much to infuse is finally decided by the parent company with global strategy deployment in mind and with the bargaining power of its subsidiaries.

As we analysed before (Figure 7.5), thus, MNC subsidiaries' SO strategy, ST strategy, WO strategy and WT strategy are heavily influenced by the restraints of role mechanism and the availability of parenting advantage.

# Strategic system for MNC subsidiaries

The strategic system of MNC overseas subsidiaries' growth and development comprises different levels of growth and development activities. Based on the analysis results of S-SWOT, MNC subsidiaries can consider what activities they want to engage in and how these activities can generate consolidated effects. This is the process of strategy-crafting for achieving synergies and integration from the high-level to the low-level activities and corporation. Therefore, the study of MNC subsidiaries' growth and development strategic system is also an important aspect of the theoretical study of MNC subsidiaries' growth and development.

## *Layers and structure of strategic system*

Any firm's growth and development strategic system is formed by coordination, interaction and support of different strategic layers. The same is true for MNC overseas subsidiaries' growth and development strategic system, which includes three levels: corporate layer, operation layer and function layer. Each layer consists of a number of growth and development activities (Figure 7.6).

### Corporate layer strategy of overseas subsidiaries' growth and development

The corporate function of overseas subsidiaries is the highest-level strategy in the system of overseas subsidiaries' growth and development. It refers to the game plan to accomplish the

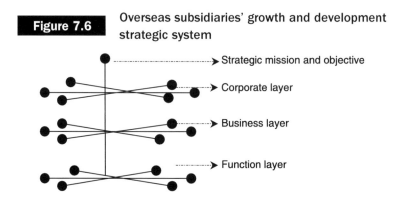

**Figure 7.6** Overseas subsidiaries' growth and development strategic system

mission and strategic goals assigned by the parent company. The core of corporate-level strategy is mission-driven under the role mechanism restriction. The dominant strategy differs for each subsidiary depending on its role. For example, the dominant strategy for resource-oriented overseas subsidiaries is usually to obtain access to the host country's tangible resources; the dominant strategy for production bases overseas subsidiaries is to secure cheap labour and land resources in the production process to reduce the cost of products; and the dominant strategy for market expansion overseas subsidiaries is to seek potential markets with greater capacity.

Apart from the dominant strategy, MNC overseas subsidiaries have supporting activities to adapt to the growth and development needs in the host country and to achieve the strategic goal assigned by the parent company. Consequently, corporate-level strategy includes the following aspects:

1. Given its internal capabilities, resource status and competitive position in the external market, MNC subsidiaries have three growth and development modes: internal growth mode, external development mode and cooperative development mode. The corresponding strategy includes joint venture, mergers and acquisitions, and strategic alliance. Overseas subsidiaries may pursue vertical, horizontal and hybrid direction growth. The

corresponding strategies include market penetration strategy, market development strategy, product exploitation strategy, forward integration strategy, backward integration strategy, vertical integration strategy, related and non-related diversification strategy, consolidation strategy and contraction strategy.

2.  MNC subsidiaries need to have the right moves to cultivate localisation and core competences to gain competitive advantages in the host country with the leverage of technology transfer and management transfer from the parent company.

3.  To gain access to parenting advantages, MNC subsidiaries can adopt the coordinated strategy to work with the parent company and other subsidiaries.

4.  The generic strategy required is one that can fit in the host country environment and can deal with competition from local and other MNC firms. Depending on its dominant position in the host country market and the parent company's expectations, the MNC overseas subsidiary can adopt an overall offensive strategy, selective offensive strategy, active defence strategy, survival strategy, and competitive harassment strategy in order to sustain its leadership position or advantage position, or to maintain the status quo or disadvantaged status position as needed.

## Business strategy of MNC overseas subsidiaries

Each business unit of MNC subsidiaries needs to shape its business strategy so that it can be suitable for its industry environment, life cycle and competitive conditions. The business-level strategy of MNC subsidiaries is also controlled by the company in resource allocation.

## Functional strategy of MNC overseas subsidiaries

The functional strategy of overseas subsidiaries is the plan of functional activities for different departments, such as R&D strategy, human resource management strategy, financial strategy, production strategy and marketing strategy to implement business strategy and win competitive advantages in the host country.

Function-level strategy will change along with the evolution of overseas subsidiaries' roles and the adjustment or alteration of overseas subsidiaries' business units. A strategic business unit needs multiple functional strategies to generate the desired results. The selection mechanism differs depending on the parent company's overall strategic intent.

## Synergistic and strategic coordination of overseas subsidiaries' growth and development strategic system

Strategic autonomy for each subsidiary differs depending on its strategic role in the system. Meanwhile, for every MNC overseas subsidiary, coordination and flexibility are critical tools for the growth and development strategic system required to respond in a timely manner to the environment changes and the competitors' strategic adjustment.

While selecting the growth and development business strategies, both the parent company and the overseas subsidiaries must pay special attention to systematic coordination among all the strategic units in the MNC network. The goal of strategic coordination is to identify, create and maintain a long-term competitive advantage. The ultimate goal is the synergistic effect, to maximise the multiplying efficiency for consolidating results. In the process of growth and development, MNC overseas subsidiaries need to endure pressures from the economic situation at home and in the host country, competition from market forces, and global integration and strategic adjustment of the parent company. The strategic coordination of overseas subsidiaries functions at three levels.

## Coordination in MNC global strategy

This is the coordination between the parent company and all the MNC subsidiaries in the MNC network. Global perspective is created, nurtured and infused in the blood of every strategic business unit in the MNC network. Knowing why and how to institutionalise global perspective is critical for the MNC's success in achieving interaction or synergistic effects from all the activities among all the strategic business units. If overseas subsidiaries seek self-interest at the expense of other units or, worse, at the expense of global coordination, the MNC will lose its very foundation.

Strategic direction and corresponding responsibilities must be clear to each overseas subsidiary for implementation and measurement in each field of the MNC. Global integration can be achieved through close communication between overseas subsidiaries and headquarters staff, but local responsive strategy requires overseas subsidiaries to have relatively high independence or autonomy. Therefore, the key is to maintain an appropriate balance or trade-off between the subsidiaries' autonomy and centralised parental control (Prahalad and Doz, 2001).

## Coordination between overseas subsidiaries

At this level, both the headquarters and all the subsidiaries ensure a good coordination system to link all the subsidiaries together and achieve consolidated working efficiency for the MNC as a whole.

From the resource perspective, overseas subsidiaries share resources. They work together to coordinate their activities in R&D, production equipment, sales and marketing to achieve the economy of scale and the supply of materials at different links of production for cost leadership.

Another way to achieve synergy effects is sharing of knowledge and professional skills or proprietary mutual transfers to build better internal core competences in manufacturing, marketing and other fields.

## Coordination for functional strategies amongst MNC subsidiaries

This is the lowest level of coordination, but the most complicated one since it is a combination and composite of all the activities in the MNC network. Only when coordination of functional activities is well in place can the synergistic interactions of the network be achieved.

The strategic role determines the allocation and supply of resources, which in turn determines the growth and development of MNC overseas subsidiaries. Hence, good coordination is needed for the growth and development of the strategic system and strategic role mechanism of the overseas subsidiaries.

The coordination of activities at different levels of strategic system is ongoing under the influence and constraints of MNC strategic mission and strategic objectives. As delineated in Figure 7.6, the strategic mission and strategic objectives are not components of three layers of overseas subsidiary strategies, but they are the core of the subsidiaries' growth and development strategic system. The corporate integration strategy, business interactive strategy and function implementation strategy all move along this axis for the effectiveness and efficiency of the MNC network.

# Strategic posture of MNC overseas subsidiaries

The integration and coordination of overseas subsidiaries' growth and development strategic system is greatly influenced and restrained by the host country environment and role mechanism. Subsidiaries show different strategic postures and orientations in their growth and development strategies in reaction to environment and role changes.

In the process of development in the host country, MNC overseas subsidiaries may decide to take an active approach or a passive approach for their growth to match their core competences and capabilities with environmental changes in both the host country and home country of the parent company. There are three strategic postures for MNC overseas subsidiaries: developmental posture, stability posture and retreat posture. Each is a strategic response to the strategic challenges.

## Developmental strategic posture

Developmental strategic posture is a dynamic strategic trend in which MNC subsidiaries have gained a dominant position in competing with other firms. This posture occurs at the entry and growth phases of the life cycle. MNC overseas subsidiaries make the best use of the MNC parenting advantages and localisation advantages to rapidly expand their business and increase their market size and operation scale in the host country. Developmental strategic posture is often created by diversification, M&A, and market penetration and product development strategies.

## Stability strategic posture

Stability strategic posture is a strategic move, with which the overseas subsidiaries dealt with a disadvantageous or weak competitive position in the host country. Many overseas subsidiaries in the maturity stage adopt such a strategic posture, which can be further divided into negative posture and positive posture.

Negative stability posture is an effort to maintain the status quo. We often see that after an MNC global strategy adjustment, the strategic position of Chinese subsidiaries declines because these subsidiaries are no longer in the centre of the spotlight for the MNC network and are neglected in the global resource allocation system. These firms, restricted by their role mechanism, have to do their best to hold their position in the host country.

Positive stability posture is a form of transition from maintenance situation to the developmental stage. MNC subsidiaries proactively seek new growth opportunities from parenting advantages or from the host country to complete another strategic change or organisational change in the subsidiary, while maintaining their current competitive position. Besides, MNC overseas subsidiaries can use the host country as leverage for business or organisation restructuring and market integration. Internally, they can adopt an austerity strategy to enhance the firm's core capabilities and competitive advantages.

## Retreat strategic posture

Three major events put MNC subsidiaries in a very vulnerable situation: 1) industry maturity or saturation can put subsidiaries into the wane stage; 2) the wrong strategic choice and/or strategy implementation errors seriously impact the performance of the overseas subsidiaries; 3) overseas subsidiaries' lack of readiness under the pressure of the parent company's global strategic adjustment can totally destroy their normal operations. Bankruptcy, liquidation or disinvestments may result from the strategic retreat posture for MNC subsidiaries.

Strategic postures are the comprehensive responses of overseas subsidiaries to changes in the internal and external situation. Subsidiaries differ in their choice of postures depending on their strategic intent and leadership determination. The life cycle and competitive conditions vary in different industries and thus MNC strategic business units select a corresponding strategic posture with the help of S-SWOT analysis.

## Implications for practice and further research

The findings of this research are helpful for managers to understand the problems encountered by MNC subsidiaries and to find alternatives for dealing with the challenges.

MNC subsidiaries in China are facing two challenges: (1) focus on network efficiency in integration for the parenting advantages and strategic role expectations; (2) to cope with high demand of the host country environment and do a good job in localisation. They are striving to build a capable organisation with distinctive competencies for internal strategic position and for competing with other MNC subsidiaries.

Global competition creates a dilemma between changing product/market scope and changing distinctive competences. MNC subsidiaries in most industries are inflexible in changing the product/market scope because business diversification demands huge capital investment. To survive, MNC subsidiaries must invest a considerable amount of energy and effort in improving distinctive competences and in upgrading their technology so that they can have stronger strategic status in the MNC system.

This study modelled the challenge–response behaviour of MNC subsidiaries in China involved in global integration and host localisations. The conceptual framework focused on the flow of challenge, perception and response of MNCs and their overseas subsidiaries facing multiple strategic challenges. By capturing the dynamic aspects of the challenge–response behaviours, the model helped guide research on MNC Chinese subsidiaries in a fast-changing environment.

## Implications for policy-makers

The results will also help policy-makers in government and strategic managers in business to better understand the behaviour of MNC subsidiaries in China, in the face of strong global competition and social, economic and industrial changes.

Our findings suggest that the primary role mandate given by MNCs to their subsidiaries in China is to be low-cost production centres for their global operations. In the case of Japanese and Korean MNCs, the production from China is primarily exported back to the home nations, with a potential to support value-added production destined for international markets. In case of US and European MNCs, the production from China is being used to develop and penetrate the Chinese domestic market and to similarly support value-added production in the home bases and other regional bases of the MNCs. A greater degree of strategic autonomy in a greater range of functional areas, and within each functional area, is evident in situations where the MNC subsidiaries in China are focused more on the domestic market. Conversely, in situations where the MNC subsidiaries are focused more on playing the role of a global factory, they have to work with greater levels of parental control and lower levels of localisation.

Historically, the policy of the Chinese government has put

priorities on exports and on promoting China as a cost-effective base for global production and market needs. The findings of our study suggest that the export-oriented policy may be at odds with another important policy goal of the Chinese government: to seek an upgrade of the technological capabilities of the China-based operations of MNCs. As long as MNCs see Chinese subsidiaries primarily as a low-cost base and as a global factory, they will like to maintain their strategic control over their subsidiaries. Thus, as the findings of the study show, most Chinese subsidiaries remain dependent for knowledge and technology and other critical resources primarily on the parent company. The flow of knowledge is predominantly one way – from the parent company to the Chinese subsidiaries. Conversely, when MNCs see Chinese subsidiaries as strategic options to develop and penetrate the Chinese market too, they are more willing to support the development of autonomous competitive capabilities of these subsidiaries. Such Chinese subsidiaries also become more capable of reciprocation with original knowledge development and sharing of that knowledge with the parent company and with other subsidiaries in the MNC network.

Until recently, the policy of the Chinese government has been to offer access to the Chinese market as a carrot in order to induce MNCs to share more sophisticated know-how with their Chinese subsidiaries. Foreign MNCs continue to face significant barriers in accessing the Chinese market. The general policy perception is that if foreign MNCs are offered a freer access to the Chinese market, they will destroy or acquire the local enterprises and will not support the technological growth of China. The findings of the present research suggest a need to revisit these policy assumptions. Freer access to the Chinese market might actually enable Chinese subsidiaries to develop new knowledge bases, based on the unique cultural and historical endowments of China, in order for them to compete effectively in the local market. In order to benefit from these new knowledge bases, MNCs are likely to provide greater strategic autonomy to Chinese subsidiaries and, over time, also be willing to more openly share know-how with them as part of a bilateral or even multilateral system of knowledge exchange throughout the MNC network. All of this should significantly expand the imports of knowledge endowments into China and help complement its national trade surplus in physical goods.

# References

Bao Mingxin, Chen Xiaoyue, Mo Lixun and Rosenzweig, P.M. (1999) *International Management: Text and Cases*. Beijing: China Machine Press, 117.

Bartlett, C.A. (1983) MNCs: Get Off the Reorganization Merry-Go-Round. *Harvard Business Review*, March–April: 138–46.

Bartlett, C.A. and Ghoshal, S. (1986) Tap Your Subsidiaries for Global Reach. *Harvard Business Review*, 64(6): 87–94.

Bartlett, C.A. and Ghoshal, S. (1989) *Managing Across Borders: The Transnational Solution*. Boston: Harvard Business School Press.

Birkinshaw, J. (1997) Entrepreneurship in Multinational Corporations: The Characteristics of Subsidiary Initiatives. *Strategic Management Journal*, 18(3): 207–29.

Birkinshaw, J. (2001) *Strategy and Management in MNE Subsidiaries*. London: Oxford University Press.

Birkinshaw, J. and Hood, N. (1997) An Empirical Study of Development Processes in Foreign-owned Subsidiaries in Canada and Scotland. *Management International Review*, 37(4): 339–64.

Birkinshaw, J. and Hood, N. (1998a) *Multinational Corporate Evolution and Subsidiary Development*. New York: St. Martin's Press.

Birkinshaw, J. and Hood, N. (1998b) Multinational Subsidiary Evolution: Capability and Charter Change in Foreign-Owned Subsidiary Companies. *Academy of Management Review*, 23(4): 773–95.

Birkinshaw, J. and Morrison, A.J. (1995) Configurations of Strategy and Structure in Subsidiaries of Multinational Corporations. *Journal of International Business Studies*, Fourth quarter: 729–53.

Birkinshaw, J., Hood, N. and Jonsson, S. (1998) Building Firm-Specific Advantage in Multinational Corporations: The Role of Subsidiary Initiative. *Strategic Management Journal*, 19(3): 221–41.

Boddewyn, J.J. (1979) Foreign Divestment: Magnitude and Factors. *Journal of International Business Studies*, 10(1): 21–7.

Boddewyn, J.J. (1983) Foreign and Domestic Divestment and Investment Decision: Like or Unlike? *Journal of International Business Studies*, 14: 23–6.

Bowman, E. and Hurry, D. (1993) Strategy Through the Option Lens: An Integrated View of Resource Investments and the Incremental Choice Process. *Academy of Management Review*, 18(4): 760–82.

Brandt, W.K. and Hulbert, J.M. (1976) Patterns of Communication in the Multinational Corporation: An Empirical Study. *Journal of International Business Studies*, Spring: 17–30.

Buzzell, R. (1968) Can You Standardize Multinational Marketing? *Harvard Business Review*, November–December, 49: 102–13.

Caves, R.E. (1998) Industrial Organization and New Findings on the Mobility and Turnover of Firms. *Journal of Economic Literature*, 36(4): 1947–82.

Chandler, A.D. (1962) *Strategy and Structure*. Cambridge, MA: MIT Press.

Chandler, A. (1987) *Visible Hand-American Enterprise Management Revolution*. Beijing: The Commercial Press.

Chopra, J., Boddewyn, J.J. and Torneden, R.L. (1978) U.S. Foreign Divestment: A 1972–1975 updating. *Columbia Journal of World Business*, Spring: 14–18.

Contractor, F. and Lorange, P. (1988) *Cooperative Strategies in International Business*. Lexington, MA: Lexington Books.

Cooke, W.N. (1992) Product Quality Improvement Through Employee Participation: The Effects of Unionization and Joint Union-management Administration. *Industrial and Labor Relations Review*, 46: 119–34.

Delaney, E. (1998) Strategic Development of Multinational Subsidiary in Ireland. In: J. Birkinshaw and N. Hood (eds) *Multinational Corporate Evolution and Subsidiary Development*. London: Macmillan, 239–67.

Douglas, S.P. and Wind, Y. (1987) The Myth of Globalization. *Colombia Journal of World Business*, Winter: 19–29.

Du, Z. and Tang, W. (2002) Comparative Research of Small and Medium Enterprises' Development Environment in China and America. *Journal of Beijing Institute of Machiner*, 3.

Dunning, J.H. (1977) Trade Location of Economic Activity and the Multinational Enterprise: A Search for an Eclectic Approach. In: B. Ohlin, P.O. Hesselborn and P.J. Wiskman (eds) *The International Allocation of Economic Activity*. London: Macmillan.

Dunning, J.H. (1981) *Ownership-Specific Advantages: International Production and Multinational Enterprise*. London: George Allen and Unwin, 80–1.

Dunning, J.H. (1988) *Explaining International Production*. London and Boston: Unwin Hyman.

Dunning, J.H. (1993) Introduction: The Nature of Transnational Corporation and Their Activities. In: J.H. Dunning (ed.) *The Theory of Transnational Corporations, The United Nations Library on Transnational Corporations*. London and New York: Routledge.

Egelhoff, W.G. (1980) *Matrix Strategies and Structures in Multinational Corporations*. Paper presented at the Academy of International Business Annual Meeting, New Orleans.

Elinder, E. (1961) How International Can Advertising Be? *International Advertiser*, December: 12–16.

Etemad, H. and Dulude, L.S. (1986) *Managing the Multinational Subsidiary*. London: Croom Helm.

Fang, Z. (2000) *Enterprise Competitive Advantage*. Taiwan: Prospect Enterprise Management Ltd. Press.

Forsgren, M. and Johanson, J. (1992) *Managing Networks in International Business*. Philadelphia: Gordon and Breach.

Forsgren, M. and Pederson, T. (1998) Centers of Excellence in Multinational Companies: The Case of Denmark. In: J. Birkinshaw and N. Hood (eds) *Multinational Corporate Evolution and Subsidiary Development*. London: Macmillan, 141–61.

Franko, L.G. (1971) *Joint Venture Survival in Multinational Corporations*. New York: Praeger.

Ghoshal, S. and Nohria, N. (1989) Internal Differentiations Within Multinational Corporations. *Strategic Management Journal*, (10): 323–37.

Ghoshal, S. and Nohria, N. (1993) Horses for Courses: Organizational Forms for Multinational Corporations. *Sloan Management Review*, 34(2): 23–35.

Ghoshal, S. and Westney, D.E. (eds) (1993) *Organization Theory and the Multinational Corporation*. New York: St. Martin's Press.

Gu, Z. (2000) Core Competitive Competence of Small and Medium Enterprises and Strategic Research of Enterprise Growth. *Economic Problems*, 10: 25–7.

Gupta, A.K. and Govindarajan, V. (1991) Knowledge Flows and the Structure of Control Within Multinational Corporations. *Academy of Management Review*, 16(4): 768–92

Gupta, A.K. and Govindarajan, V. (1994) Organizing for Knowledge Within MNCs. *International Business Review*, 3(4): 443–57.

He, J. and Zhang, H. (2004) Research and Development on the Problem of Marketing Internationalization and Localization in China. *Journal of Beijing Technology and Business University.*

Hedlund, G. (1980) The Role of Foreign Subsidiaries in Strategic Decision Making in Swedish Multinational Corporations. *Strategic Management Journal,* 11(1): 7–22.

Hedlund, G. (1981) Automony of Subsidiaries and Formalization of Headquarters-Subsidiary Relations in Swedish MNCs. In: L. Otterbeck (ed.) *The Management of Headquarters-Subsidiary Relationships in Multinational Corporations.* Aldershot: Gower.

Hedlund, G. (1986) The Hypermodern MNC: A Tetrarchy? *Human Resource Management,* 25: 9–36.

Hillman, R. and Soden, J.V. (1973) How to Market a Divestment. *McKinsey Quarterly,* 9(4): 52–9.

Hood, N. and Yang, S. (1990) *Multinational Company Economics.* Beijing: Economic Science Publishing House.

Hulbert, J.M. and Brandt, W.K. (1980) *Managing the Multinational Subsidiary.* New York: Holt, Rinehart and Winston.

Hymer, S.H. (1966) *The International Operations of National Firms: A Study of Direct Foreign Investment.* Doctoral dissertation. Boston: MIT.

Jarillo, J.C. and Martinez, J.I. (1990) Different Roles for Subsidiaries: The Case of Multinational Corporations in Spain. *Strategic Management Journal,* 11(7): 501–12.

Kim, W.C. and Mauborgne, R.A. (1993) Effectively Conceiving and Executing Multinationals' Worldwide Strategies. *Journal of International Business Studies,* 24(3): 419–48.

Kitching, J. (1974) Winning and Losing with European Acquisitions. *Harvard Business Review,* 52(2): 124–36.

Kogut, B. and Kulatilaka, N. (1994) Options Thinking and Platform Investment: Investing in Opportunity. *California Management Review*, 36(2): 53–71.

Kojima, K. (1977) *Study on Foreign Direct Investment*. Tokyo: Japan Diamond Press.

Kojima, K. (1987) *Theory of Foreign Trade*. Tianjin: Nankai University Press.

Kong, S. (2001) *International Direct Investment*. Beijing: University of International Business and Economics Press.

Kottler, P., Fahey, L. and Jatusripitak, S. (1985) *The New Competition*. Englewood: Prentice-Hall.

Levitt, T. (1983) The Globalization of Markets. *Harvard Business Review*, May–June, 61: 92–102.

Li, W. and Li, B. (2003) The Analysis on Multinational Corporations' Inclination in Investing in China: From the Perspective of Share Structure Strategy. *Management World*, 1: 57–62.

Li, X. (2002) Entrepreneurship, Entrepreneurial Competence and Enterprise Growth – International Seminar of Entrepreneurial Theory and Enterprise Growth. *Economic Research*, 1.

Li, Z. (2002) Basic Routes of Enterprise Growth in the New Century. *Research on Economics and Management*, 3: 29–32.

Lin, C. (1984) *Plural Nationality Enterprise*. Taiwan: Wunan Press.

Liu, Y. and Chen, R. (2001) Competency-based and Enterprise Growth Strategy. *Research on Economics and Management*, 4.

Lorange, P.A. (1976) Framework for Strategic Planning in Multinational Corporations. *Long Range Planning*, June: 30–7.

Lorenzoni, G. and Baden-Fuller, C. (1995) Creating a Strategic Center to Manage a Web of Partners. *California Management Review*, 37(3): 146–63.

Malnight, T.W. (1996) Transition from Decentralized to Network-based MNC Structures: An Evolutionary Perspective. *Journal of International Business Studies*, 27: 43–65.

Mao, Y. (2005) *Multinational Corporations' Investment Strategy in China*. Beijing: China Financial and Economic Publishing House, 54.

Markides, C.C. (1995) Diversification, Restructuring and Economic Performance. *Strategic Management Journal*, 16: 101–18.

Markides, C.C. and Berg, N.A. (1992) Good and Bad Divestment: The Stock Market Verdict. *Long Range Planning*, 25(2): 10–15.

Martinez, J.I. and Jarillo, J.C. (1989) The Evolution of Research on Coordination Mechanism in Multinational Corporations. *Journal of International Business Studies*, 20(3): 489–514.

Mehrdad, B. (1999) *The Alchemy of Growth*. Beijing: Economic Science Press.

Moore, K.J. and Birkinshaw, J.M. (1998) Managing Knowledge in Global Service Firms: Centers of Excellence. *Academy of Management Executive*, 12(4): 81–92.

Moore, K.J. and Heeler, R.A. (1998) Globalization Strategy for Subsidiaries – Subsidiary Specific Advantages. *Journal of Transnational Management Development*, 3(2): 1–14.

Myers, S. (1977) Determinants of Corporate Borrowing. *Journal of Financial Economics*, 5(2): 147–75.

Osland, G.E. and Yaprak, A. (1994) Learning Through Strategic Alliances. *European Journal of Marketing*, 29(3), 52–67.

Otterbeck, L. (1981) The Management of Joint Ventures. In: L. Otterbeck (ed.) *The Management of Headquarters-Subsidiary Relationships in Multinational Corporations*. Aldershot: Gower.

Pan, Z. and Lu, M. (2003) Route Dependence of Small and Medium Enterprises Growth Strategic Choice. *Economic Management*, 16: 4–11.

Paterson, S.L. and Brock, D.M. (2002) The Development of Subsidiary-Management Research: Review and Theoretical Analysis. *International Business Review*, 11(2): 139–63.

Perlmutter, H.V. (1969) The Tortuous Evolution of the Multinational Corporation. *Columbia Journal of World Business*, 4 (January–February): 9–18.

Porter, M.E. (1976) Please Note the Location of Nearest Exit: Exit Barriers and Planning. *California Management Review*, 19: 21–33.

Porter, M.E. (1986) *Competition in Global Industries*. Boston: Harvard Business School Press.

Porter, M.E. (1990) *The Competitive Advantage of Nations*. New York: The Free Press.

Porter, M.E. (1991) America's Green Strategy. *Scientific American*, April.

Prahalad, C.K. and Doz, Y. (1981) An Approach to Strategic Control in MNCs. *Sloan Management Review*, 22(4): 5–14.

Prahalad, C.K. and Doz, Y.L. (1987) *The Multinational Mission, Balancing Global Integration with Local Responsiveness*. New York: Free Press; London: Collier Macmillan.

Prahalad, C.K. and Doz, Y. (2001) *The Multinational Mission*. Translated by: Binwen Wang. Beijing: Hua Xia Publishing House.

Putti, J.M. and Harold, H.W. (1999) *Principles of Management*. Beijing: China Machine Press.

Randoy, T. and Li, J. (1998) Global Resource Flows and MNE Network Integration in Development. In: J. Birkinshaw and N. Hood (eds) *Multinational Corporate*

*Evolution and Subsidiary Development*. New York: St. Martin's Press, 76–101.

Rivoli, P. and Salorio, E. (1996) Foreign Direct Investment and Investment under Uncertainty. *Journal of International Business Studies*, 27(2): 335–57.

Sachdev, J.C. (1976) *A Framework for the Planning of Divestment Policies for Multinational Companies*. Unpublished Doctoral Dissertation. University of Manchester, England.

Schuler, R. and Walker, J. (1990) Human Resources Strategy: Focusing on Issues and Actions. *Organizational Dynamics*, 19(1): 5–19.

Solberg, C.A. (2000) Educator Insights: Standardization or Adaptation of the International Marketing Mix: The Role of the Local Subsidiary/Representative. *Journal of International Marketing*, 8(1): 78–9.

Stopford, J.M. and Wells, L.T. (1972) *Managing the Multinational Enterprise*. New York: Basic Books.

Subhash, C.J. (1989) Standardization of International Marketing Strategy: Some Research Hypotheses. *Journal of Marketing*, 53: 70–9.

Surlemont, B.A. (1998) Typology of Centers Within Multinational Corporations: An Empirical Investigation. In: J. Birkinshaw and N. Hood (eds) *Multinational Corporate Evolution and Subsidiary Development*. New York: St. Martin's Press, 162–88.

Taggart, J.H. (1996) *An Empirical Evaluation of the C-C Paradigm*. SIBU Working Paper 96/6, University of Strathclyde.

Taggart, J.H. (1997) An Evaluation of the Integration-Responsiveness Framework: MNC Manufacturing Subsidiaries in the UK. *Management International Review*, 37(4): 295–318.

Taggart, J.H. (1998) Strategy Shifts in MNC Subsidiaries. *Strategic Management Journal*, 19(7): 663–81.

Taggart, J.H. (1999) MNC Subsidiary Performance, Risk, and Corporate Expectations. *International Business Review*, 8(2): 233–55.

Tao, X. and Zhao, S. (2003) Demonstration Research on the Influence of Subsidiary Company's Role and Performance to Multinational Corporation's Localization of Human Resources. *Management World*, 8: 92–8.

Taylor, M.L. (1988) *Divesting Business Units: Making the Decision and Making It Work*. Lexington, MA: Lexington Books.

Teng, W., Huang, Y. and Zhang, Y. (1992) *Multinational Corporation Strategic Management*. Shanghai: Shanghai People Press.

Tornden, R.L. (1975) *Foreign Divestment by Multinational Corporations: With Eight Case Studies*. New York: Praeger.

Tyebjee, T.T. and Bruno, A.V. (1984) A Model of Venture Capitalist Investment Activity. *Management Science*, 30(9): 1051–66.

Udo, Z. and Kogut, B. (1995) Knowledge and the Speed of the Transfer and Imitation of Organizational Capabilities: An Empirical Test. *Organization Science*, 6: 76–92.

UN Multinational Corporation Center (1994) *1993 World Investment Report*. Beijing: Foreign Trade Education Press.

Vernon, R. (1966) International Investments and International Trade in the Product Cycle. *Quarterly Journal of Economics*, 80: 190–207.

Vernon, R. (1974) The Location of Economic Activity. In: J.H. Dunning (ed.) *Economic Analysis and the Multinational Enterprise*. New York: Praeger, 89–114.

Vernon, R., Wells, L.T. and Rangan, S. (2000) *The Manager of the International Economy*. (7th edition). Beijing: Tsinghua University Press.

White, R.E. and Poynter, T.A. (1984) Strategies for Foreign-owned Subsidiaries in Canada. *Business Quarterly*, 48(4): 59–69.

Wiseman, R.M. and Gomez-Mejia, L.R. (1998) A Behavioral Agency Model of Managerial Risk Taking. *Academy of Management Review*, 25: 133–52.

Wu, A., Jia, S. and Chen, H. (2003) Conversion of Entrepreneurial Competence and Family Enterprise's Development and Replacement in the Process of Enterprise Growth. *Foreign Economies and Management,* 6: 20–4.

Wu, Wenwu (2000) *New Theory of Multinational Corporation.* Beijing: Beijing University Press.

Xi, Y. (2002) *Multinational Corporation Management.* Beijing: China Machine Press.

Xiao, S. (2003) Dialysis on Internal Trade of Multinational Corporation's Subsidiary Company in China. *Commercial Economy and Management,* 10: 40–3.

Yang, Y. and Nengzhi, J. (1999) Analysis on the Instability of Joint Venture Enterprise. *Investment Research,* 5.

Yang, Z. (2000) *Research on Multinational Corporation's Control Mechanism on Joint Venture Enterprise.* Nanjing: School of Commerce of Nanjing University.

Youssef, S.M. and Hulbert, J. (1975) Contextual Factors Influencing Control Strategy of Multinational Corporations. *Academy of Management Journal*, March: 136–43.

Zanfei, A. (2000) Transnational Firms and Changing Organization of Innovative Activities. *Cambridge Journal of Economics*, 24: 515–54.

Zhang, R. (1998) *Research and Development Strategy.* Guangzhou: Guangdong Economy Press.

Zhang, X. (2003) Product Lifecycle Management Influences Enterprise Growth. *China Enterprise News.*

Zhao, J. (1996) *International Operation of Modern Corporation.* Jinan: Shandong People Press.

Zhao, J. (1998) Comparative Research on Wholly Foreign-owned Enterprise in China. *State Education Commission Funds Task Report.*

Zhao, J. (1999a) Comparative Research on the Operating Mode of the Subsidiary Company of America, Japan and Korea. *The Selected Works of the Second World Management Forum.*

Zhao, J. (1999b) *International Comparison on Enterprise Management-Comparison, Reference and Innovation of Chinese, Japanese and American Enterprise Management.* Jinan: Shandong People Press.

Zhao, J. (2002) *Strategic Research on Multinational Corporation's Subsidiary Company in China.* Beijing: Economic Management Press.

# Index

Printed in the United States
By Bookmasters